CBD. Will It Work For Me?

The Power and Pitfalls of CBD. A Consumer's Guide.

Matthew Burch and Jonathan Howkins, CBD Genie
www.cbdgenie.uk

CBD eXtra

If you're new to CBD, or if you've tried it, but not achieved the results or outcomes you were looking for, then this may be just right for you.

We've teamed up with a small, select number of CBD brands to bring you the best quality CBD products on the UK market, at the lowest price.

We'll not only be reviewing these products ourselves, but also getting your views, opinions and feeback as well.

Sound interesting?

You can find more details on our website: **cbdgenie.uk/cbd-extra** or by scanning the QR code below on your phone or mobile device which will take you directly to our website.

SCAN ME

Please Note:

The opinions expressed in this book are those of the authors and contributors alone and should not be taken as advice or instructions. If you have any questions or doubts about taking CBD, you should seek the advice of a medical professional.

Additionally, if you are currently taking any medication or are pregnant you should consult with your medical professional before taking CBD.

First published in May 2023.

ISBN 978-1-7393875-0-1

@cbdgenie

@cbdgenie.uk

@cbdgenie

Before we get started...

If you're interested in learning more about how CBD is helping others just like you, then do join our community on Facebook.

This is a great place to ask questions and also share your own experiences.

We've created this unbiased Group so that we can all learn more about the ever-changing CBD market in the UK.

We'll be adding to the Group on a regular basis; sharing stories, reviews and interviews, so it's a great place to get the latest on new CBD products, as well as real-world experiences and support.

Join the Group

There's full details on the website at:
cbdgenie.uk/facebook-group

or simply scan the QR code.

SCAN ME

Acknowledegements

We would like to thank the many people we've had the opportunity to talk to and learn from over the last 12 months, as we've immersed ourselves in the world of CBD.

With every conversation we've gained more knowledge and insights into this amazing compound and the industry, along with the innovators seeking to provide support and a natural solution to their health conditions.

It's been an inspiring journey so far, hearing the enthusiasm that comes both from within the CBD industry and from those who are having their health and wellbeing transformed by it.

We would like to say a special thank you to our eight 'CBD Experts' featured in this guide. These individuals truly embody everything you'd want from a CBD brand in terms of expertise, integrity, and passion.

Thank you for your openness, honesty and unique perspective:

Rowan Bailey from Infinity CBD

Paul Batchelor from Herbotany Health

Ben Birrel from CBD Brothers

Jess Cohen and Sophie Garner from Canax Life

Paul Finnegan from Naturecan

Oren Landa from Kiara Naturals

Matt McNeill from Kloris CBD

Jade Proudman from Savage Cabbage

You can learn more about each these people and their CBD brands later in this guide.

Would you write a short review?

If you have any comments or feedback for us about any aspect of this book we'd love to hear from you. Please contact us via our website: cbdgenie.uk

And if you enjoy this guide and find it useful and informative, we'd really appreciate it if you could write us a short review on Amazon. It only takes a couple of minutes, but it's hugely valuable to us, as we try to reach more people who could benefit from CBD.

Write a Review

You can leave your review by visiting:
www.cbdgenie.uk/book-review
or simply scan the QR code to vist our
website where you'll find full details.

Thank you - we really do appreciate you
taking the time to do this.

Your quick reference guide

As you'll see, this guide is structured into a number of sections, to make it easier for you to dip in and out and find what you're looking for.

At the end of each section, we've provided both links and QR codes so you can continue learning or access additional resources.

Here's a brief summary of what's in this guide:

Section 1 is for you if you're interested in learning a little more about why this book has been written.

Section 2 is helpful if you're totally new to CBD and want to understand the fundamentals of the hemp plant and some background to this amazing compound.

In Section 3, you can learn directly from leading CBD experts as they answer the Top 20 questions we identified that consumers have.

Section 4 will help you to learn more about our CBD Experts, their brands and their product portfolios.

In Section 5, we've collated our ten tips for assessing your CBD products to ensure you're getting the best quality, experience, and value for money from your purchase.

In Section 6, we share three CBD Stories, where individuals walk through their personal experiences of trying CBD and how it's helped them address their health issues.

Finally, in Section 7, we've outlined some additional resources and reference points for those wishing to go deeper into the world of CBD.

Throughout the Book we've also provided QR codes and website links to provide you with additional information, resources and videos etc.

Contents

SECTION ONE

CBD: Will it work for me?

A big welcome from us.

We came to CBD as beginners, as novice consumers curious and hopeful for something being regarded as a wonder solution to many health and wellness issues.

We each arrived on a different path but found that we both had an enthusiasm to explore CBD and figure out what it was and how it might help us, as well as everyone else.

For Jonathan, trouble sleeping had been his constant companion for over 20 years, so any real help was going to be a huge magnet. For Matt, his interest in medicinal cannabis, although not for himself, was already rooted, but a CBD client wanting their products photographed was the catalyst to start him on his CBD journey.

It was conversation at lunch after a networking meeting that birthed the idea of working together to create a learning platform for consumers. Jonathan's background in digital marketing was combined with Matt's, at the time, madcap idea for a YouTube channel. This started to form a frame for where both of us could go in terms of exploring CBD, and sharing that journey with everyone.

Between us we had the tools. Jonathan was able to craft the website and start the process of reaching out to the CBD market. Matt's photography studio became the YouTube studio and without much planning, we started filming ourselves sampling CBD tea in January 2022.

We were a couple of novices in the world of CBD and YouTube (still are!) but we had a vision, of sorts.

By April 2022, we were at the CBD Show in London as 'roving reporters' interviewing exhibitors and learning about their products, their companies and the future of CBD and the market.

This was a turning point for us in that we felt we had found a groove and that bridging the gap between the 'expert' level CBD brand owners and information-hungry consumers, was our mission.

That sounds like we thought of ourselves as trailblazers! We didn't and don't, as there are lots of fantastic advocates for CBD, many of whom we are learning from. In fact, this book has been partly created by talking with CBD experts.

Our perspective and standpoint is that of an interested consumer. We're not looking to be experts, but prefer to view the market with some objectivity, curiosity and maybe a little cynicism.

A core component of this book is the '20 Questions' we posed to our eight CBD experts, which we originally shot as extended interviews on our YouTube channel.

Because, let's face it, having your questions answered by the very people producing CBD products, in some cases actually growing the hemp as seed to shelf operations, has got to be weightier than us!

We've learned from them and are now sharing their opinions and knowledge with you. You can read their abbreviated answers in this book, or watch and listen to the entire interview on YouTube. Either way, you'll be better informed on CBD and ready to start your journey.

There's also our website www.cbdgenie.uk, which is another fantastic resource for you to explore. The site has an expanse of articles, information and a growing list of CBD companies in the UK, about which we have done a deep dive giving you a profile of each of them and we hope this helps you on your journey.

Once you've read the book we hope you'll be inspired to share your experiences with using CBD. You'll find links to do this in our CBD Stories section.

We all have a long way to travel with CBD as a companion and we're excited to see where it takes us.

If you want to keep in touch then subscribe to our YouTube channel, follow us on Instagram and Facebook, sign up to our newsletter on our website, and send us feedback.

We hope you enjoy this book and find the answers you are looking for as you embark on your CBD journey.

Let us know.

Matt & Jonathan

Our intention is to provide help, support, and guidance.

This book is intended to help consumers navigate the world of CBD. To better understand where it comes from, how it's produced, the benefits, the potential negatives, a sense of the UK market, and how to find the right product for you.

We do not intend for this book to be a comprehensive encyclopaedia of CBD, rather a practical guide so you can plan where to start your journey with answers to some of the basic questions.

Who's it for?

The statement 'it's for everyone' is often used, but it *can* be said that it is for everyone, at least those wanting clear information on CBD and those who want to learn about the benefits and have a guide to the market.

You might be looking for something to help with pain, anxiety or sleep problems. You may be in good health but interested in a natural complementary wellness product, wanting to ease or prevent future health issues. You may have a family member or friend who needs something for an ailment.

Regardless of your situation we hope these pages offer some enlightenment.

What will it do for you?

Ideally when you read this book, the veil of mystery will be lifted. You will feel confident to choose your CBD products and have an understanding of how CBD might help you.

The new world of CBD has seen the launch of many new products in a very short time and the market can be overwhelming. There are many questions even within the industry. So as a consumer, it is understandable that you will have your own questions.

We hope that these pages go a long way to answering your questions and give you the information you need to make your decision about starting your journey with CBD.

But if you feel we've missed anything then please let us know.

Just to be clear, this is not a definitive work.

OK, neither of us are health professionals, nor do we have a background in the CBD world. This book is intended as a consumer's guide written by learning consumers with the involvement of CBD experts.

It should be taken as a guide to help you explore CBD further. It is not a definitive work, nor is it a medical book. At every step, check in with your doctor, especially if you are on medication or pregnant.

The world of CBD is in flux and as we progress, details will need updating. How the market will look in five years will be very different to today. We journey through a changing landscape with little cast in stone.

Once you've read the book...

Once you've been through this guide, we would suggest visiting our website cbdgenie.uk and explore the variety of companies we've listed. We drill into what the company is about, their products, and their customer feedback ratings.

You can also subscribe to our YouTube channel, CBD Genie, where we continue to add interviews, product reviews and industry news. It's a great resource and we've ambitious plans for the future to help share information and connect with CBD enthusiasts from around the globe.

CBD UK Brands

Visit the CBD Genie website to explore the range of CBD brands:
www.cbdgenie.uk/cbd-directory

Or scan the QR code.

Subscribe on YouTube

Subscribe to our YouTube Channel
@cbdgenie for the latest product news, reviews and interviews.

SECTION TWO

CBD Fundamentals

In this section of the book we dive into the fundamentals of CBD and explore What it is, What's in it and How it works. Plus the legal and regulatory framework that's helping to bring great transparency and trust into the market.

What is CBD?

We need to start by dealing with the elephant in the room. CBD does come from the cannabis plant. Yes, you read that correctly. Cannabis. So, let's take a look at the details and dig into what that means.

If you Google CBD/hemp/cannabis or any variety of search pertaining to cannabis, you will possibly be confused. Website after website offers explanations as to the varieties of cannabis and how they relate to CBD.

Initially, you may think you have a clear handle on it, then you read something that muddies the waters.

We can offer a simplistic explanation.

Exploring the cannabis plant can be fascinating but it's akin to 'going down the rabbit hole'. If you feel like being Alice, grab a coffee first and maybe some biscuits, it's quite a journey.

Cannabis Sativa (C.sativa) comes in two main varieties, with one producing high levels of THC (tetrahydrocannabinol) and the other producing high levels of CBD (cannabidiol).

THC is the psychoactive compound which causes the 'high' people experience. This variety of cannabis is commonly called marijuana, grass, weed, reefer, pot, doobie, hash and others, with THC levels averaging around 15%.

THC levels have greatly increased over the years. In the 1970s THC strength was around 3%, so the weed today certainly carries more punch, with some strains containing up to 30% THC.

It's important to appreciate these relative percentage strengths because they underpin the entire UK's legal position with CBD.

If the cannabis plant seed contains less than 0.2% THC then it is classed as Industrial Hemp. It is this Industrial Hemp plant that contains the high levels of CBD.

CBD is not psychoactive, addictive, hallucinogenic or a controlled substance. It is believed to have a wide range of health benefits and can be taken in many forms, making it readily available to the consumer.

CBD in its raw state is a viscous oil extracted from the hemp plant which is then processed in various ways to produce a consumer friendly product, for example a palatable oil, gummies, skin creams, and beverages.

The cannabinoids can be found in the whole of the Hemp plant, but the highest concentration is in the flowers and secondly the leaves.

Once the 'crude oil' has been extracted from the plant, it can be put through additional processes to separate the various compounds which leads to creation of the three main varieties of CBD.

Full Spectrum CBD

This is when all the compounds extracted from the hemp plant are included in your CBD product. This full range of compounds, including the THC, terpenes and flavonoids, are thought to have positive and complementary benefits, creating what is referred to as an 'entourage effect' which we'll look at shortly.

Broad Spectrum CBD

Basically, broad spectrum CBD is similar to the Full Spectrum, but without the THC. For many people wary of THC in any quantity, this is the ideal option. You retain the potential 'entourage effect' with the other compounds, but your product is THC free.

CBD Isolate

CBD Isolate is the purest form of CBD, as it contains only the cannabidiol compound, with all other plant material, terpenes, and cannabinoids removed. This makes it ideal for those who want to experience the potential benefits of CBD without any other components from the cannabis plant. However there is no 'entourage effect'.

There is a fourth version of CBD, which is synthetically created. In this instance the CBD compound is replicated entirely in a lab. The benefits of this are that it is very consistent and not reliant on growing plants, or extracting oils. However this could also be considered its weakness, as it's not organic in any way.

Under current UK law, growers of industrial hemp must apply for a licence via the Home Office, who control and monitor the industry very closely. Growing hemp in the UK without a licence is illegal, even a single plant in your garden.

But despite being able to grow hemp, farmers or anyone else cannot extract the cannabinoids in the UK, meaning that the raw CBD oil has to be imported.

UK companies import CBD extracts and oils from the United States, Switzerland, Portugal, and The Netherlands, to name a few.

Hopefully this will change in the coming years, so that UK farmers can grow and sell the flowers (and indeed the whole plant) for cannabinoid extraction and CBD.

This would undoubtedly give a useful and long term boost to the farming industry.

Notably, the Channel Islands have been licensing hemp for cannabinoid extraction and we understand the UK Government is watching with interest.

Why does CBD work?

CBD works by interacting with the endocannabinoid system. The endocannabinoid system (ECS) is a complex cell-signalling system found in the bodies of all mammals, including humans. It was discovered in the early 1990s during research into the effects of cannabis on the human body. Since then, scientists have found that the ECS plays a crucial role in maintaining overall balance and homeostasis in the body by regulating various physiological processes.

The endocannabinoid system consists of three main components:

Endocannabinoids: These are naturally occurring compounds that are similar in structure to the cannabinoids found in the cannabis plant, such as CBD and THC. The two most well-studied endocannabinoids are anandamide (AEA) and 2-arachidonoylglycerol (2-AG).

Receptors: Endocannabinoids bind to specific receptors found throughout the body, primarily the CB1 and CB2 receptors. CB1 receptors are predominantly found in the brain and central nervous system, while CB2 receptors are more commonly found in the immune system, peripheral nervous system, and other tissues.

Enzymes: These are responsible for breaking down endocannabinoids once they have fulfilled their function. The main enzymes involved in this process are fatty acid amide hydrolase (FAAH) for anandamide, and monoacylglycerol lipase (MAGL) for 2-AG.

The endocannabinoid system plays a role in a wide range of physiological processes, including mood regulation, appetite, immune response, pain management, memory, and sleep.

When the body experiences an imbalance or stress, the ECS works to restore homeostasis by producing endocannabinoids, which bind to the CB1 and CB2 receptors and trigger various responses.

Cannabinoids from the cannabis plant, such as CBD and THC, can also interact with the endocannabinoid system.

These compounds have been found to have potential therapeutic effects in various medical conditions, including chronic pain, anxiety, epilepsy, and multiple sclerosis, among others. However, more research is needed to fully understand the mechanisms and long-term effects of cannabinoids on the ECS and human health.

How does CBD work with the human endocannabinoid system?

CBD interacts with the human endocannabinoid system (ECS) in several ways, which may contribute to its observed benefits.

For example, CBD has been found to bind to serotonin receptors (5-HT1A), which are involved in regulating mood, anxiety, and sleep. This interaction may contribute to some of the observed effects of CBD, such as reduced anxiety and improved sleep quality.

CBD has also been shown to interact with CB2 receptors, which are primarily found in the immune system. By binding to these receptors, CBD may help modulate immune responses, reduce inflammation, and provide relief for conditions such as chronic pain and autoimmune disorders.

It's important to note that while the interaction of CBD with the human endocannabinoid system is promising, more research is needed to fully understand its mechanisms, potential benefits, and long-term effects.

How is CBD made?

Your CBD product might have been bought from a company operating a seed to shelf business or one buying a CBD concentrate and then making their end product. You may have bought a 'white label' CBD product where one company makes the product to sell to another company to retail under their label.

Creating the CBD that goes into your products, involves multiple processes. It's the unseen 'how it's made' that can be fascinating but also good to know if you're essentially eating the end product.

Cannabis is a plant, so it starts at the farm. A large amount of care goes into the selection of the seeds, the farming process, harvesting, drying, and care of the plant material used for CBD extraction, which is mostly the flowers, but can include the leaves. It takes 8-9 months from seed to harvest.

Science and art, with love and a prayer to the weather gods, combine to deliver a quality crop. Then, science takes over, as what is needed are the microscopic compounds extracted from the plant material in a usable form.

There are several methods for extracting CBD (cannabidiol) from the cannabis plant, each with its advantages and disadvantages. The main goal of these extraction processes is to isolate the CBD in its purest form while leaving behind unwanted plant materials and impurities. The most common CBD extraction methods are:

CO2 Supercritical Extraction: This method uses carbon dioxide (CO2) in its supercritical state, where it exhibits properties of both a liquid and a gas, to act as a solvent and extract the desired compounds. This method is known for producing a high-quality, pure, and concentrated CBD extract. It is also considered environmentally friendly, as CO2 is a non-toxic substance and can be recycled after the extraction process.

Ethanol Extraction: In this method, ethanol is used as the solvent to extract CBD from the cannabis plant. This technique is generally considered safe and efficient, as ethanol is a polar solvent that can effectively dissolve a wide range of compounds. However, the extraction process may also dissolve unwanted substances like chlorophyll, which can lead to a less pure final product. Further purification steps, like winterization and filtration, can be employed to enhance the quality of the CBD extract.

Hydrocarbon Extraction: This process utilises hydrocarbon solvents, such as butane or propane, to extract CBD from the cannabis plant. While this method can produce a highly potent and pure CBD extract, it also comes with potential risks, as hydrocarbon solvents are flammable and can leave behind toxic residues if not properly purged from the final product.

Olive Oil Extraction: This is a simple and cost-effective method that involves decarboxylating the cannabis plant material (heating it to activate the cannabinoids) and then infusing it in olive oil. While this method is safe and easy to perform at home, it results in a less concentrated CBD extract, and the final product has a shorter shelf life compared to extracts obtained using other methods.

Cold Press Extraction: Although not commonly used for CBD extraction, cold press extraction can be employed to obtain hemp seed oil, which has its own set of benefits. This method uses mechanical pressure without heat or solvents, resulting in high-quality oils that maintain their natural characteristics.

Each CBD extraction method has its pros and cons, and the choice of technique depends on factors such as the desired purity, concentration, and intended use of the final product, as well as the available equipment and budget.

What are Terpenes and Flavinoids?

In addition to CBD, there are a number of other compounds within the oil extracted from the hemp plant, which can contribute to the overall benefits and outcomes.

The main ones are Terpenes and Flavinoids, which as discussed before are present in both the Full Spectrum and Broad Spectrum CBD, but not in the Isolate.

Terpenes

Terpenes are a large and diverse class of organic compounds that are naturally produced by a wide variety of plants, including the cannabis plant, as well as some insects. They are the primary constituents of essential oils and are responsible for the characteristic aroma and flavour of many plants, fruits, and flowers.

In the cannabis plant, Terpenes are produced in the trichomes, which are the same glandular structures where cannabinoids like THC and CBD are synthesised. There are over 100 different terpenes identified in the cannabis plant, and each strain has a unique Terpene profile that contributes to its distinct aroma and flavour.

Some of the most common Terpenes found in the cannabis plant include:

Myrcene: This Terpene has an earthy, musky aroma and is also found in plants like hops, thyme, and mango. It is believed to have potential anti-inflammatory and analgesic effects.

Limonene: As the name suggests, limonene has a strong citrus aroma and is commonly found in citrus fruits. It has been associated with potential mood-enhancing, anti-anxiety, and anti-inflammatory properties.

Pinene: This Terpene has a characteristic pine-like aroma and is also found in pine needles, rosemary, and basil. Pinene is thought to have potential anti-inflammatory, bronchodilator, and memory-enhancing effects.

Linalool: Linalool has a floral, lavender-like scent and is found in lavender, coriander, and many other plants. It is often associated with potential calming, anti-anxiety, and pain-relieving properties.

Caryophyllene: This Terpene has a spicy, peppery aroma and is also found in black pepper, cloves, and cinnamon. Caryophyllene is unique among Terpenes because it can directly bind to CB2 receptors in the endocannabinoid system, suggesting potential anti-inflammatory and analgesic effects.

In addition to their aromatic properties, Terpenes are thought to have various potential therapeutic effects, and some studies suggest that they may work synergistically with cannabinoids in a phenomenon we previously mentioned which is the "entourage effect." which we'll come onto next.

Flavonoids

Flavonoids contribute to the plant's overall chemical profile and are responsible for some of the plant's colors, as well as providing potential health benefits.

There are over 20 different flavonoids identified in the cannabis plant, with some of the most common ones being cannflavin A, cannflavin B, and quercetin.

These flavonoids, like those in other plants, exhibit antioxidant, anti-inflammatory, and anti-microbial properties. They may also contribute to the potential therapeutic effects of cannabis and hemp-derived products, including CBD oil.

Some CBD products, which include either Full Spectrum or Broad Spectrum CBD oil, contain a variety of cannabinoids, terpenes, and flavonoids from the whole cannabis plant, which contribute to the 'entourage effect'.

On the other hand, products with CBD isolate contain only purified CBD and do not have the accompanying terpenes and flavonoids.

The choice between these types of products depends on individual preferences and desired effects.

What is the 'Entourage Effect'?

The entourage effect is a concept in cannabis and hemp research that suggests the various compounds found in these plants, including cannabinoids, terpenes, and flavonoids, work together synergistically to produce more significant therapeutic benefits than each compound would on its own.

In other words, the combined effects of these compounds are more potent and effective than the sum of their individual effects.

The cannabis plant contains over 100 different cannabinoids, including THC (tetrahydrocannabinol) and CBD (cannabidiol), as well as various terpenes and flavonoids that contribute to its overall chemical profile.

These compounds are believed to interact with one another and with the human endocannabinoid system in complex ways, leading to the entourage effect.

For example, some studies have suggested that certain terpenes may enhance the therapeutic effects of cannabinoids or modulate their psychoactive effects.

Similarly, the combination of CBD with other cannabinoids and terpenes might lead to improved anti-inflammatory, analgesic, and anxiolytic effects, among others.

The entourage effect is an important consideration when choosing cannabis or hemp-derived products, such as CBD oil.

Is hemp seed oil the same as CBD hemp oil?

Hemp seed oil and CBD hemp oil are not the same, although they both come from the hemp plant (Cannabis sativa). They differ in their source within the plant, their composition, and their uses.

Hemp seed oil is extracted from the seeds of the hemp plant, typically through cold pressing. It is rich in essential fatty acids, such as omega-3 and omega-6, as well as various nutrients and vitamins. However, hemp seed oil contains little to no cannabinoids like CBD or THC. It is widely used in cooking, skincare products and as a dietary supplement due to its nutritional value.

On the other hand, CBD hemp oil is extracted from the flowers, leaves, and stalks of the hemp plant, where cannabinoids like CBD are predominantly found.

Can I grow hemp in my garden?

NO. Hemp can only be grown under licence from the Home office. Farmers or hemp growers have to comply with various criteria to qualify for a licence and one is issued for every crop. Even then, CBD cannot be extracted in the UK and has to be imported.

What about CBG, CBC and CBN?

In addition to CBD, you may also come across other compounds with similar names, such as CBG, CBC and CBN.

There are more than 120 identified cannabinoids found in the Cannabis plant.

CBG (cannabigerol), CBN (cannabinol), and CBC (cannabichromene) are just three of these. They each have unique properties and potential therapeutic benefits.

Here's a brief overview of each and how they differ from CBD (cannabidiol):

CBG (Cannabigerol):

CBG is considered the "parent" cannabinoid because it acts as a precursor to other cannabinoids. Most of the Cannabigerol is converted into other cannabinoids, including CBD, THC, and CBC during the plant growth.

It is non-psychoactive, meaning it does not cause the "high" associated with THC. Research on CBG is limited compared to CBD, but some studies suggest it has potential anti-inflammatory, antibacterial, and neuroprotective properties.

CBG is typically found in much lower concentrations in mature cannabis plants than CBD or THC.

CBN (Cannabinol):

CBN is a mildly psychoactive cannabinoid formed as a by-product of THC degradation. It is usually present in small amounts in aged cannabis plants.

CBN has attracted interest for its potential sedative and sleep-promoting effects, as well as its potential anti-inflammatory, antibacterial, and neuroprotective properties.

CBN is not as well-researched as CBD, and its effects are thought to be more subtle.

CBC (Cannabichromene):

CBC is another non-psychoactive cannabinoid derived from CBG. Research on CBC is also more limited than CBD, but some studies suggest it may have anti-inflammatory, analgesic (pain-relieving), and antidepressant properties.

CBC is thought to work synergistically with other cannabinoids through the "entourage effect," enhancing the overall therapeutic potential of cannabis.

In Summary

In summary, while CBG, CBN, and CBC are all cannabinoids found in the cannabis plant, they differ from CBD in their chemical structures, concentrations in the plant, and potential therapeutic effects.

Each cannabinoid has unique properties, and ongoing research aims to better understand their individual and combined benefits for medical applications.

Using CBD

How does it work?

Before we start there's one important caveat - and that is no CBD company or brand can claim that their products have actual medicinal benefits.

CBD is classified as a food and as such, is sold as a wellbeing product not dissimilar to supplements. Claims of how CBD can help you have to be based on anecdotal evidence only.

In terms of what is known, whilst the research is ongoing, CBD complements the human body's endocannabinoid system with people reporting improvements to sleep patterns, pain management, general wellbeing, calming anxiety issues, and more.

What CBD products can I buy?

Any time that question is answered, the answer is out of date. Since 2017 in the UK, there has been an explosion of products containing CBD and the list keeps growing. As more research is done, as more markets are explored the list will likely keep on growing.

At present the most well-known products are oils, gummies, vapes, patches, balms, chocolate and teas. But there are also more innovative CBD products now on the market such as honey, beer, wine, and soft drinks.

Having said the above, no new ingestible products can be offered to the market until the FSA allow further applications for a Novel Food Licence.

CBD Bioavailability: Why is it important?

CBD bioavailability refers to the proportion of CBD that enters the bloodstream and becomes available for the body to use when a CBD product is consumed.

In other words, bioavailability determines how much of the ingested CBD is absorbed and can produce its desired effects. The higher the bioavailability, the more efficiently the CBD is absorbed and utilised by the body.

Bioavailability is an essential factor to consider when using CBD products, as different methods of consumption and product formulations can lead to varying degrees of absorption and outcomes.

The main methods of CBD administration include:

Oral ingestion: When CBD is consumed orally, such as in the form of capsules, edibles, or oils, it must pass through the digestive system and liver before entering the bloodstream. This process, known as the first-pass metabolism, can reduce CBD bioavailability, with estimates ranging from 4% to 20%.

Sublingual administration: CBD can be absorbed directly into the bloodstream through the mucous membranes under the tongue by using sublingual products such as tinctures, sprays, or lozenges. This method bypasses the first-pass metabolism and typically results in higher bioavailability, ranging from 12% to 35%.

Inhalation: When CBD is inhaled through methods like vaping or smoking, it enters the bloodstream rapidly through the lungs, offering the highest bioavailability, which can range from 34% to 56% or even higher. However, this method may not be suitable for everyone due to potential respiratory concerns.

Topical application: CBD can be applied topically in the form of creams, balms, or lotions. Topical CBD typically does not enter the bloodstream but instead interacts with local cannabinoid receptors in the skin. This method is suitable for addressing localized issues, such as joint pain or skin inflammation.

To improve CBD bioavailability, some products use advanced formulations, such as nanoemulsions or liposomal delivery systems, which can enhance the absorption of CBD and make it more readily available for the body to use.

Is there a limit to how much I should take?

70 mg of CBD has been set as a maximum daily recommended dose by the Food Standards Agency and subsequently the industry as a whole. However, it is a contentious issue.

What makes this dosage seem arbitrary is that the maximum recommended dose suggested on some websites in the US is anything up to 600 mg.

CBD is a natural product which is helping a lot of people with health issues. The nature of CBD and how it interacts with the body is that it seems more of an art than a science. People with sleeping issues will report different dosages as the optimum amount.

So, focusing on sleep, some people may find restful nights on 20 mg a day, some may need 70 mg a day, and some may need more.

There is no clinical evidence to suggest higher levels of CBD should be harmful. In fact, when studies are conducted, subjects receive massively higher levels.

Can I overdose on CBD?

Essentially, no. There is no evidence to suggest you can overdose on CBD. The THC levels are so low as to not be a factor, and the other compounds don't work in such a way as to add up to an overdose. We have to leave room for the possibility that individuals may have an adverse reaction to CBD, perhaps in high quantities. But as of now, overdosing isn't a concern.

Will I experience cannabis highs with CBD?

No, not in the sense that you will with marijuana and high levels of THC. You may experience a calming, restful reaction, but not a high.

Can I still drive when taking CBD?

This question is an interesting one. Fundamentally yes, but any driver is responsible for ensuring they are in full control of their faculties and responses and fit to drive. If CBD makes you feel in any way unfit to drive, then clearly you should refrain.

Is CBD addictive?

No evidence has been put forward to suggest that CBD is addictive.

Are there different CBD dosage recommendations for men and women?

No, except that some will argue that body mass and general physical size may be a factor, but then personal endocannabinoid systems are likely more of a determining factor.

Will CBD show up during a work drug test?

Cannabidiol (CBD) is a non-psychoactive compound found in cannabis plants. Most workplace drug tests are designed to detect the presence of tetrahydrocannabinol (THC), which is the psychoactive component in marijuana that causes the 'high' feeling. CBD itself should not show up on a standard drug test.

However, there are some caveats to consider:

Product quality and labelling: CBD products may contain trace amounts of THC, depending on the source and extraction process. Some products might be mislabelled or have higher THC levels than advertised, leading to a positive test result for THC.

Cross-reactivity: In rare cases, some drug tests may yield false-positive results due to cross-reactivity with other cannabinoids present in the CBD product. This is more likely with lower-quality drug tests.

High doses of CBD: Consuming large amounts of CBD could potentially result in the accumulation of small amounts of THC in your system, which might be enough to trigger a positive result on a drug test.

It is essential to choose reputable, high-quality CBD products with transparent, accurate labelling to minimise the risk of THC contamination.

If you are concerned about drug testing at work, consider discussing your CBD use with your employer or human resources department to clarify their policy and address any concerns.

Does CBD make you tired or sleepy?

CBD (cannabidiol) is known for its potential therapeutic effects, but its impact on sleepiness or tiredness can vary depending on the individual and the specific product used.

Some people report that CBD helps them feel more relaxed, which could lead to a sense of calmness and potentially improved sleep. However, others may not experience any sedative effects.

However, research on this topic is still limited, and more studies are needed to establish a clear relationship between CBD and sleep.

It's important to note that individual reactions to CBD can vary, and factors such as dosage, the specific type of CBD product used (e.g. full-spectrum, broad-spectrum, or isolate), and the method of consumption (e.g. oil, capsule, or edible) can all influence its effects.

Can CBD cause anxiety?

CBD (cannabidiol) is generally considered to have calming and anxiolytic (anti-anxiety) properties.

Several studies have shown that CBD may help alleviate anxiety in various contexts, such as generalised anxiety disorder, social anxiety disorder, and anxiety related to post-traumatic stress disorder (PTSD).

However, individual reactions to CBD can vary, and in some rare cases, people might experience increased anxiety or other side effects.

A few factors can contribute to the increased anxiety after using CBD:

Dosage: The appropriate dosage of CBD can vary for each individual. Some people may experience increased anxiety if they take too much or too little CBD. It's essential to start with a low dose and gradually increase it until the desired effects are achieved.

Product quality: Low-quality or contaminated CBD products can contain harmful substances or higher levels of THC (tetrahydrocannabinol) than advertised, which might contribute to anxiety.

Individual factors: Each person's body chemistry and endocannabinoid system are unique, and individual reactions to CBD can vary

Can I vape CBD?

Yes, you can vape CBD. Vaping is one of the many ways to consume CBD, and it has gained popularity because it typically provides faster effects compared to other methods like ingestion or topical application.

When you vape CBD, it is absorbed directly into the bloodstream through the lungs, allowing for a more rapid onset of effects.

To vape CBD, you'll need a vaporizer device and CBD vape products such as vape juice, vape oil or CBD-infused e-liquids. These products are specifically designed for vaping and are not the same as CBD oil tinctures, which are meant for oral or sublingual consumption.

When choosing a CBD vape product, it's essential to select a high-quality, reputable brand to ensure the product is safe and free from contaminants.

Please note that while vaping CBD is considered generally safe, inhaling any substance into your lungs carries some level of risk. If you have any concerns about vaping or using CBD, consult with a healthcare professional to discuss the potential risks and benefits based on your individual needs and medical history.

CBD: The Legalities

A potted history of hemp across the world and specifically the UK

CBD is being treated as a Novel Food because it has been chemically extracted from the hemp plant and has therefore become something new. However, the source of CBD is hemp and that is not new, most definitely not to the UK.

Hemp can be traced quite possibly to the beginning of civilisation. It has been in many ways a constant companion for humans. Hemp first appeared around 10,000 years ago in Asia but has been found over Europe, Africa, and South America.

Over the millenniums, it has been used for oil, pottery, clothing, shoes, ropes, food, building materials, paper, biofuel, and even an experimental car body by Henry Ford in the 1940s. Hemp is without doubt an incredible plant.

If you're wondering whether hemp is a new plant crop in the UK, in 1533, Henry VIII made it law that farmers had to grow hemp for ropes, sails, and clothing, so the fields of England were literally covered with hemp!

However, in 1928 the UK banned hemp growing when hemp was caught up in the legal purging of cannabis. This might seem, given that hemp contains less than 0.3% THC, unfair and it does seem to perhaps be the root of why we have restrictions on growing and cultivating the hemp plant.

What bodies, authorities or organisations are dealing with CBD in the UK?

In the UK, several regulatory bodies and organisations oversee the CBD industry to ensure product safety, quality, and compliance with legal requirements.

Some key authorities and organisations involved in the regulation and oversight of CBD products include:

Food Standards Agency (FSA): The FSA is responsible for regulating the safety and quality of food products in the UK, including CBD products marketed as food supplements or additives. The FSA has established guidelines for CBD products, including Novel Food regulations, which require manufacturers to submit safety assessments and gain authorization before selling their products.

Medicines and Healthcare products Regulatory Agency (MHRA): The MHRA regulates medicines, medical devices, and related products in the UK. If a CBD product is marketed with medicinal claims or intended for therapeutic use, it may be classified as a medicine, and the MHRA will oversee its regulation and approval.

Home Office: The Home Office is responsible for the licensing and enforcement of cannabis-derived products, including the cultivation and production of industrial hemp. They regulate the legal THC limits in CBD products and ensure compliance with the Misuse of Drugs Act.

Trading Standards: Local Trading Standards authorities enforce consumer protection laws and ensure that CBD products are accurately labelled, safe, and compliant with legal requirements.

Cannabis Trades Association: A membership-based organisation in the UK representing businesses operating within the legal cannabis and hemp sectors, including the CBD industry. The CTA aims to promote good practices, provide support to its members, and ensure the industry's compliance with legal and regulatory requirements.

Are the laws/regulations the same across the whole UK?

The FSA covers England, Wales, and Northern Ireland. In Scotland, the role is performed by Food Standards Scotland (FSS)

Is CBD legal and regulated in the UK?

Yes. In a nutshell, CBD is legal in the UK and has been since 2017, provided that the THC level is below 0.2% in the final product.

There is some ambiguity over THC and various people in the industry offer slightly different positions on this aspect.

We're not lawyers, so our commentary on this should be taken as our interpretation but the wording on the Home Office's website suggests that the allowance of 0.2% THC is given only in relation to the seed...

"There needs to be a defined commercial end use and the Home Office only issues licences for cultivation of plants from approved seed types with a THC content not exceeding 0.2%. The '0.2%' reference is used solely to identify varieties which may potentially be cultivated, within the scope of this policy..."

It seems that this particular legislation fails to exert specific detail regarding the end product - ie the CBD must not exceed 0.2% THC. This omission potentially allows CBD, even with a small amount of THC, to possibly be legal under the Home Office guidance, or illegal under the Misuse of Drugs Act 1971.

This impacts Full Spectrum CBD products, which are readily available through retailers in the UK. There seems to be two camps of thought. Some say any trace of THC would deem the product illegal and others hold to the 0.2% as being the legal threshold.

Clearly the FSA are also concerned that a Novel Food Product doesn't contain an illicit drug and they may deem any CBD product with any trace of THC as illegal.

The FSA's Novel Food application list is closed to new applications but at the time of our publication, no application has been certified. This means that as applications are processed, we as consumers and of course the industry will discover whether 0.2% THC in a CBD product is legally acceptable.

In 2017, CBD was made legal in the UK but at that time, it seems nobody really appreciated the impact this would have in terms of an emerging market.

Generally speaking, an industry evolves over decades, clearly in some cases hundreds of years.

Over these generational periods successive governments and authorities legislate to control and regulate these industries either for, at the basic level, public safety and security, or for taxation.

However the rapid growth of the CBD market has left the regulators and legislation trying to catch up. It's like the industry in the last six years has been born, sped through infancy, the teenage years, and is trying to enter adulthood very quickly.

The FSA is now the official body in the driving seat with regards to legislation over the ingestible CBD products and as such, companies have to submit applications for a new ingestible product under the Novel Food Act.

The reason CBD falls to the FSA as a Novel Food is because CBD is being extracted from the plant, so whilst hemp has been consumed in one form or another for thousands of years, extracted CBD is effectively a new food substance.

Before the days of the FSA and 'regulation' the market looked very different with many more brands and products being sold with little or no quality control.

When the FSA stepped in their solution was to draw a line in the sand and stop any new products being launched and then require all CBD companies to submit detailed applications together with in depth lab reports to evaluate and prove their product quality.

This was not only a complex process, but an expensive one for fledgling brand owners, many of whom were running 'cottage industry' style businesses.

Unfortunately for companies and brands that didn't make it through the validation criteria and onto the FSA's list, it was the end of the road. However on the plus side, the CBD industry was being legitimised.

Being on the FSA's list is a big deal as currently no new applications can be made, and the FSA is working to remove any products not on the list from the UK market.

As a consumer though, you should know that no company or no product has yet received approval from the FSA.

If you want to get up to date information on this approval process, you can simply search for 'FSA CBD list' to see all the brands and individual products currently being processed and evaluated.

But what of all the other products on the market: patches, balms, salves, make up, hair products, sexual health products, fabrics? They're not regulated so far as we know, so watch this space.

Can I take my CBD with me when travelling abroad?

This is probably ill-advised. The laws of the country you are travelling to or through should be examined. CBD is still illegal in some countries.

Can I buy CBD from outside the UK?

The raw CBD oil used to manufacture a retail CBD product must be purchased outside the UK since it isn't permitted to extract the cannabinoids in the UK.

To do this though, you will need at minimum an EORI number, a registered company, and an import licence. This presumes you are wanting to start a CBD business, which at the moment would be restricted to topicals or non-ingestibles.

If you are looking to purchase a CBD retail product to ingest from a CBD company abroad, the product must be on the Food Standards Agency Novel Food Application list. In other words, buying from them can be no different to purchasing from a UK company.

You cannot purchase the flowers, buds or leaves and import them to the UK.

CBD lab reports. Why would I look at them?

CBD lab reports should be available for you to review on any brands website selling CBD ingestibles, such as Oils, gummies etc.

The lab report is a document provided by an independent, third-party laboratory that ensures product quality, safety, and transparency.

It provides information on the product's composition, potency, and purity, as well as confirms that it meets industry standards and complies with regulations.

A CBD lab report typically includes the following information:

Cannabinoid profile: This section of the report lists the concentrations of various cannabinoids found in the product, such as CBD, THC, CBG, and others. It helps verify the potency and ensures that the product contains the appropriate amount of CBD and complies with legal THC limits.

Terpene profile: Terpenes are naturally occurring compounds in the cannabis plant that contribute to its aroma, flavour, and potential therapeutic benefits. The lab report may include a list of the terpenes detected and their concentrations.

Contaminant testing: The report should indicate whether the product has been tested for potential contaminants, such as heavy metals, pesticides, residual solvents, and microorganisms (bacteria, mould and fungi). This information is crucial for ensuring the product's safety and purity.

Batch information: The report should include details about the specific batch of the product tested, such as the batch number, production date, and expiration date.

Are there recommended age restrictions for CBD use?

Most companies recommend CBD not be taken by the under 18s.

Why might CBD be non-advised if I am pregnant?

Just about every CBD product you buy will warn against taking CBD if you are pregnant. From what we have discovered, this largely errs on the side of caution, as there is little evidence either way of the effect CBD has on a foetus. Until there is more research producing verified evidence it would be wise to avoid CBD whilst pregnant.

Are there any side effects with CBD?

It depends how you define side effects. People take CBD to help with sleeping issues, but if your CBD chills you to the point of unwanted sleepiness, then you might think of this as a side effect.

That said, there is no solid evidence to date that there are negative side effects from taking CBD.

There are anecdotal experiences which suggest some people have diarrhoea, dizziness and nausea, but it isn't widespread, and no authority has been alerted to medical conditions via A&E.

We've heard the term 'desired and undesired effects' as opposed to 'side effects'. The reason you're taking CBD is generally because you're seeking a specific wellness benefit, so your desired effect might be someone else's undesired effect.

Can I use CBD if I am breastfeeding?

For much the same reason as it's recommended to avoid CBD whilst pregnant, it is currently advised that you should not take CBD if you're breastfeeding.

Until more research has been done on the potential transference of CBD via breastfeeding to a baby it's advisable to avoid CBD whilst breastfeeding.

Where is the best place to buy CBD?

We have posed this question in one form or another to our experts and you can read their answers later in this book.

However the main thing to consider is that if you're wanting to buy CBD to consume or use on your body, it follows that you want to seek reputable products from reputable retailers.

Investing a little time on research will be time well spent as there are many factors to consider and definitely some things to avoid.

We go into this in more detail in our Top 10 Tips later in this book, so make sure you check that out.

Are CBD products tested on animals?

Some CBD companies may test their products on animals during the research and development phase to assess the safety and efficacy of their formulations. However, many CBD companies have adopted a cruelty-free approach and do not use animal testing.

In recent years, there has been a growing trend towards cruelty-free and ethical practices in the cosmetics and wellness industries, which has led to more companies opting for alternative testing methods. These alternatives may include in vitro testing, computer simulations, or human clinical trials.

If you want to ensure that the CBD products you purchase have not been tested on animals, look for certifications or statements from the manufacturer that indicate their commitment to cruelty-free practices.

Conversely, CBD is now being used to treat animals and can be prescribed by vets.

However it's currently illegal to give your pets CBD that you've purchased for yourself and there are no CBD products specifically for pets available through retail channels in the UK.

CBD products are essentially formulated for human consumption and a pet's dosage requirement and indeed type of CBD, would be different to that of a human.

Is it legal to grow CBD plants in the UK?

Only with a licence from the Home Office. We have seen cases in the press where people have argued that their cannabis, industrial hemp or otherwise, is legal because CBD is legal.

Do not make this mistake. It is illegal to grow any type of cannabis plant (which includes hemp) in the UK without a Home Office licence.

What if I see hemp products being sold at local markets?

There are many small CBD manufacturers who make use of local markets to sell their CBD products. All you need to do is check if the company is on the FSA Novel Food Application List. If they are on the list awaiting approval, they are a legitimate CBD business.

Are there hemp farms I can visit?

There are hemp farms in the UK, but their locations are not readily made public. If you're particularly interested in visiting a CBD production hemp farm, you should simply approach the company in the UK directly and ask.

SECTION THREE

Ask The Experts

In this section of the book we've sought the advice and opinions of eight of the UK's leading CBD experts and brand owners.

We asked them what we believe are the 20 most common questions consumers ask when looking to try or buy CBD.

CBD Experts on YouTube

Check out the interviews with our CBD Experts on our YouTube channel
@cbdgenie.uk

Or scan the QR code.

SCAN ME

What can be treated with CBD?

Whilst CBD companies are not allowed to make any medical claims, the response below represents the reality of why people are exploring CBD as an alternative or complementary, therapy or treatment.

Sophie & Jess @ Canax Life

Okay, so in our experience, we've got sleep anxiety, stress, pain relief, and it's great as an anti-inflammatory for skin conditions and hormone balance. Most of our reviews on our website are for sleep issues where it really, really does help, which then has a knock effect with stress and anxiety.

Ben@ CBD Brothers

Anxiety is one of our top ones. Arthritis is another one. We have a lot of people with Parkinson's, and we have various different forms that go on. But they're the most common ones that we're obviously not allowed to 'treat' because of the rules, but if we were to be able to do that, then that would be something that we would say if we were allowed to say it!

Matt @ Kloris CBD

Well, we divide all of the products and the ranges that we do into meeting five key needs. So they revolve around sleep, anxiety, stress related issues, pain, and active skincare. Other things that we've done help with the skin and the skin biome. Then finally, menopause and menopause related symptoms. So, we focus all of our work around that and we find that those are the five key things that people come to us and say they find the most benefit from.

Paul @ Herbotany Health

Well, there's numerous reasons: general mental health, rheumatism, aches and pains from work and exercise, skin complaints, insomnia. Too many to mention.

Paul @ Naturecan

So, we are obviously not allowed to offer advice on these different specific symptoms, but for us, anxiety is one of the key ones. Insomnia and just generally not sleeping very well.

Rowan @ Infinity CBD

We are a little bit restricted with what we can say directly as medical claims, but what I can kind of comment on, is what most people come to us saying they've been referred for and it is quite a wide range.

We get customers coming in saying they've been told to try CBD for anxiety, depression, sleep, PTSD. We're also ranging up to more chronic conditions, whether it be arthritis, nerve related issues, fibromyalgia, and issues like that.

You've got people using it more temporarily here and there, for wellness, but predominantly it's mental health and chronic pain that people are being referred to CBD.

Oren @ Kiara Naturals

The most common symptoms that we see CBD is most effective on is really stress and anxiety, sleep problems, and pain. We're also seeing a lot of things that are related to inflammation, which takes us into autoimmune diseases and a bunch of other things.

But I would say that the top things that we are treating at the moment are really pain, sleep, anxiety, and stress. There's also depression, which is up and coming.

Jade @ Savage Cabbage

It's a wonderful question that's difficult to answer simply because of MHRA guidelines. So, what I would say is, I notice that a lot of my Savage Cabbage community report that they are sleeping better, they are feeling less anxious, and that they are living their lives in a way which is easier to what life was like prior to starting using the oil. (and that's how robotic I have to be, unfortunately!)

Will taking CBD replace my existing pain or anxiety medication?

Sophie & Jess @ Canax Life

Obviously, CBD is a complementary therapy. So, for medication, you'd have to speak to your GP before taking CBD with medication.

But if you can run it alongside medication, we have got some reviews from customers where CBD has helped reduce their anxiety medication or the pain medication. But I would never suggest reducing your medication without speaking to your doctor.

Ben@ CBD Brothers

I believe that it has a place and I believe that full spectrum cannabinoids will play a much bigger part. I think with anxiety, we see a lot of use with CBD that is really, really helpful, and really beneficial.

I know that THC in that mix is not particularly good. We've seen a lot of things, as I said, with Parkinson's that have been useful.

So, replace medication, yes, but it's very much dependent on the type and the severity of the condition.

There are some people we've tried to help but CBD hasn't touched the edges, which means they're left with their pharmaceuticals or in a worst case scenario with very little because the pharmaceuticals aren't working.

Matt @ Kloris CBD

We would always refer someone to talk to their GP about this before replacing any medication with CBD. What we do find is a lot of people find that CBD is extremely helpful with a lot of varying symptoms and ailments and some of those people feel that allows them to reduce other medication usage.

Yet sometimes, it's complementary to that. Sometimes, it is replacing it entirely. But it is very important that if this is an ongoing medical issue, that anything like that is done in consultation with a medical professional.

Paul @ Herbotonay Health

Personally, the benefits for myself I can answer yes. I would suggest that any potential user of CBD products, whether our brand or another, consult their GP before stopping any existing medication.

Paul @ Naturecan

What we'd say is this, you always keep your medical consultant on board with the decisions that you make with these things. But what we found, and this is symptomatic in the States as well, a lot of people that have taken strong painkillers when they've played a lot of sport, had injuries, have seen a massive reduction in those when they've taken CBD.

So that would be one that I definitely categorise as something that can definitely reduce your intake or hopefully, you know, completely kill it.

Rowan @ Infinity CBD

It can and it can't, but it's certainly never something that we can advocate without talking with your doctor, which is vital when it comes to changing or adapting or adding anything to supplements or prescriptions that you're taking.

It is certainly a leading cause for why people come to us. They're on certain medications that they've either decided long-term they don't want to be on or are having issues with side effects.

So, they're looking for an answer and many of our customers have found that with CBD. Definitely work with your doctor and make sure that you're open and honest with them about what it is that you're doing, the dosage and just make sure that you're getting their advice as well.

Oren @ Kiara Naturals

Well, CBD is being used across the world to replace or reduce medication across the board. Now I'm personally not a doctor, I'm an osteopath and naturopath, but I do work in clinical practice and I work with many other doctors supporting my patients and clients.

And we see that there is a huge space for reducing medications, especially pain, sleep, and anxiety medication with CBD.

We're also seeing some evidence on heart medication, anything to do with the cardiovascular system, and also depression in the States, where self-medication is very prominent.

There's recently been a study and they've been doing this study yearly from 2019, that among the users of CBD that use it for more than three months, 22% of them will completely replace their medication, so there's a huge potential there for CBD replacing other pharmaceutical medications.

Jade @ Savage Cabbage

My answer to that would be, we've all got an endocannabinoid system and there is research out there which suggests that if your endocannabinoid system is not functioning to the best of its ability, you will begin to notice that you've got aches and pains.

If you begin to onboard nutrition in the farm of cannabinoids, what we can see sometimes is that those issues can reduce or even disappear. I am in that category.

I am somebody who was in significant pain with a whole host of other issues, and I manage that through a very complex onboarding of cannabinoids. By complex what I mean is I swap and change how I take my oil and don't just take it at the same time every day. It's very much dependent on how I feel and I've personalised my usage to what my needs are.

Are there any known side effects with CBD?

Sophie & Jess @ Canax Life

The ones that we know of and have researched are probably a dry mouth and a difference in appetite. Maybe a bit of diarrhoea. You can sometimes, if you take the CBD on an empty stomach, maybe feel a bit sick.

The other thing to note is when taking CBD with other medication, it can interact with your medication. Especially like blood thinners and things like that. So, I would never recommend taking CBD with medication like that.

Ben@ CBD Brothers

If you take too much, I believe it can give you the runs, which isn't very good. With long-term usage, I think we saw a study, and this may have been what the Novel Food thing was based on, where if you give a mouse an amount of CBD the size of a Labrador, then it would die.

But then I think if you gave anyone that much product, they would die. So, I don't think so. I think it's a relatively safe thing in the right environment.

So, for CBD, I don't think there's a lot that can really go wrong unless something falls on your head when you're taking it or something.

Matt @ Kloris CBD

The interesting thing about CBD is if you actually look at its safety profile, it's fairly exemplary. Even like the World Health Organization has put out that, you know, they consider it to be an extremely safe substance.

There is no risk of addiction with it. It's typically very, very hard to overdose on it, although there are still ongoing studies around that because it will vary on the routes of delivery. So, there are different routes of taking CBD which offer different absorption methods.

So, it is important to be aware of the route that you are taking CBD, how that affects you, and how that may interact with any other medications that you are taking.

Other things that you are doing and particularly being wary of is, is it pure CBD you're taking? Is it a broad spectrum extract? Is it a full spectrum extract, which shouldn't be in the UK, if you're taking that, because that would then have the THC in it and that can have other unintended consequences?

So typically, what we've found from people that we've talked to who've taken CBD products of some type and have found some unintended side effects from it, that's usually been because of other adulterants in there.

Either something it's been intentionally mixed with such as the carrier oil, things like that, or it can be quite common for people to have issues with THC and that person is particularly sensitive to THC.

So even if it's very low levels, that can have unintended effects. But typically, that's where we've seen people have issues with these products.

Paul @ Herbotany Health

None that I'm aware of. Only benefits.

Paul @ Naturecan

On a couple of occasions, short term, when somebody's taken too much, they've had to go to the bathroom a little bit quicker than they've first anticipated.

A lot of these studies are going on at the moment, there was a big study with Epidialex where they found that very, very high levels over a prolonged period of taking isolate, could affect the liver. So again, there's more research being done on this, but the vast majority of research that's been done shows that CBD is more than safe.

Rowan @ Infinity CBD

Unfortunately, we could do with a lot more studies on the broad range of things that people experience with it, but obviously over the years, we've had plenty of people coming back to us with all sorts of feedback and thankfully there doesn't seem to be many common side effects that are that negative.

Some people might find that they're feeling a bit more drowsy. Some people might find that with certain strengths they feel more anxious when they're trying to not be, so more often than not, it's more to do with dosage and just trying to find a balance in the short and long term.

Dosage and tolerance can be an issue. People find that they build up a tolerance after the first month or two, especially those that are taking it more consistently with chronic conditions daily. So that can mean a larger cost or having to take much higher doses.

We are waiting to see if anything else comes through, but as it stands, it's quite positive. It definitely seems to be a better alternative to a lot of options at the moment.

Oren @ Kiara Naturals

There are known side effects. I like to refer to them more as non-desired effects, because what really is a side effect? So, for one person a side effect could be something that they want, for example, they feel tired and want to go to sleep.

For the other person that's taking it for pain, they're saying, 'Oh, I'm feeling tired, and I want to go to sleep'. That's a side effect. But the most common undesired effects that we see are really nausea and fatigue.

Some people, if they're taking full spectrums from specific strains, may get a bit more anxious or agitated. There can be headaches, depending on the quality of the CBD.

We've seen a lot of headaches coming in with gummies and things that are related to sugar. We're not sure exactly why but I would say that these are the most common ones.

Jade @ Savage Cabbage

As far as I'm aware, what I can say is that the studies that have been done, which have been part of the Novel Food submissions to the FSA, have demonstrated safety of this product.

We also are aware that a study has been done on CBD isolates, which is of course very different. And that has shown that long-term use of high strength CBD isolate can be problematic to five organs in the body and that's currently being reviewed by the authorities.

Once I start taking CBD, am I on it for the rest of my life?

Sophie & Jess @ Canax Life

Well, firstly, just so you know, CBD is not addictive.

Obviously, the THC that is addictive is removed. What I would explain to a consumer is that it's like a vitamin really. If you feel like you've got good health benefits from it, you'll obviously want to carry on taking it.

For things like sleep, if it helps with sleep, maybe if you got into a really good routine of sleep with the CBD, then you could start reducing your CBD because you've obviously got into that routine and your body has got used to that. People obviously take it as a one off. I take it for period pains, or some people take it on a daily basis. So, it all depends on the actual consumer.

Ben@ CBD Brothers

I think it's very dependent on the condition and the person that's taking it.

I mean when I have anxiety, or when I had anxiety, I would take CBD and it would level it out for a little bit and perhaps I'd go through phases with my anxiety where it would be really heightened and I'd take it more often than not, and then I'd go through periods of a couple of months where I wouldn't need to.

If someone has chronic pain and it supports them, then I suppose then yes, you'd be in a situation where you'd be taking CBD as a supplement to your medicine and that would be an ongoing thing.

I know people with certain conditions like tremors and things like that as well as epilepsy, they take it and it's an ongoing thing because it supports an existing medication.

Matt @ Kloris CBD

Absolutely not. So, I would say that the best way to think about CBD, because of the way it's interacting with the body's endocannabinoid system, is that it effectively nudges that system back into balance or into homeostasis as we call it.

You can consider it in the same way that you would consider certain vitamin supplements, so it's helping to get your body back into the state that naturally it should be in, its best self, but you don't want to form a reliance on it in that way.

We have some users who will take it every day and we have others who will just take it as and when they feel the need. It really is down to personal requirements, preferences and what you are taking it for, as well as the other things surrounding that, so 'What's causing you to take it?', 'What is the nature of the environment that you are consuming it with?'

You have to sort of look at it very much holistically for each individual.

Paul @ Herbotany Health

Not necessarily. We advise our consumers to stick with CBD for a period of time to get maximum benefits.

But I believe once you've found those benefits, I don't believe it is an issue for you to take it periodically if you are feeling moments of anxiety or increased pain. But we would recommend that you maintain a level of intake for your general wellbeing, but it's not a necessity.

Paul @ Naturecan

So, this one is different for different people. So, what I'd say is it's in no way addictive or anything like that, but for a lot of people it makes you feel so much better.

Our repeat rate at Naturecan is incredibly high. So once people start taking it, a lot of people come back and continue to take it.

And I think that's down to once you've fully engaged your endocannabinoid system and you feel better and you do stop taking it, you may notice a difference.

Because I travel a lot and in certain areas you don't want to travel with CBD, for me I feel a difference mainly in my sleep pattern, that's the biggest one for me if I stop taking it.

So, although it's not addictive, the feeling of wellness is what people want and they often keep going with it once they start taking it.

Rowan @ Infinity CBD

Everyone is different. I mean, we certainly will have customers who will probably now be on some sort of balance between CBD, or potentially end up on medicinal cannabis alongside CBD, for the rest of their lives.

Mainly the ones that were already going to be on other kinds of prescriptions for more chronic reasons, in which case it was the balance between the two.

But for many people that we work with, it seems to be a short to medium term thing to manage other issues. You know, people with anxiety perhaps who manage to break out of that balance and the repetition that's creating these things.

Maybe CBD gives them the break to address things in a different way, and that's certainly been the case for me. So, I don't think everyone will always be taking CBD.

Oren @ Kiara Naturals

Hopefully not. CBD has a great benefit of modulating the nervous system and balancing the endocannabinoid system.

So, there is already potential for a healing process within the body, not done by CBD, done by the body, but the CBD is helping to remove the barriers that are stopping that process.

We, at least at Kiara, recommend for people to take it for a time where they feel a change and always have a break because changes are happening. They might not need it and hopefully they're not, they're not going to need it.

I don't believe that any supplement or any medication should be taken for a lifetime. If you're treating the root cause, then it should be over at some point.

Jade @ Savage Cabbage

I think it's a personal choice. I mean, if you think about it from a process perspective, if you are ingesting cannabinoids, where you're topping up your endocannabinoid system or however you want to describe it, then why would you stop ultimately?

But one thing that you can also experience is strain resistance.

So, the product that you are using is no longer as effective as it once was, which is one reason we focus on just the two brands with Savage Cabbage as we tend to find a lot of our consumer base rotates the products to prevent that from happening.

Some people choose to stop and those people that I've spoken to that have chosen to stop generally come back to us within three or four months because the issues that they were dealing with prior to taking CBD have returned.

CBD is not a cure, it's not a cure for anything and neither is cannabis. And you know, that's a really important thing for people to understand, is that it is not a cure.

It is a supplement towards living your life in a way in which you feel comfortable.

Can I give CBD to my pets?

Sophie & Jess @ Canax Life

We've never really gone down this avenue.

We were kind of put off a little bit when we first started, so we've never really looked into it, but there are regulations for pets and obviously because pets can't talk, it's a different ballgame, isn't it?

I feel it would change their appetite and maybe blood pressure and things like that, so you'd have to be careful, and we're not licensed so we haven't got anything out there and we're not really thinking about it in the near future for pets.

We did have a lady that gave us some feedback that she gave her dog one of our gummies for bonfire night and it changed him, so it was the best he's ever been. There's research going on, but we've not really looked into it.

Ben@ CBD Brothers

Well, as we know, the Vets Association are not very friendly towards cannabinoids. So, they will officially say, no, you can't and no you shouldn't.

Unofficially, I've seen and know many people that give CBD to dogs with anxiety. I've seen people give it to cats with sickness.

We've got a guy who comes in, his cat has got a very severe form of cancer and it seems to be helping, it's stimulating the appetite. It's working and the cat seems to be having quite a good life.

It's not curing it, but it's definitely making its end of life a lot better.

I had a chicken that was attacked by a fox and I put balm on its back where it had been attacked and it healed up really well and never had any problems afterwards.

I can't claim that that's cannabinoids, maybe it's just my balm making skills *or maybe it was just the chicken. But I would say check with your vet, who will say no!*

Matt @ Kloris CBD

So, this is a very interesting topic and brings up some very interesting things about, particularly UK law, but also this extending to other countries as well.

At the root, every mammal has an endocannabinoid system, which is ultimately what CBD is affecting and interacting with and helping to stimulate.

Obviously and to start with, animals are a fraction of the size, generally, of humans so if they were to take it, then the dose that they would require would be correspondingly much, much smaller than a human dose.

But actually, in the UK, you can only legally give a pet CBD if you have a prescription from a vet. So, it would be a veterinary prescription, but you are not allowed to market CBD as a veterinary product in the UK as it is classed as a veterinary medicine.

Basically, it's not legal to market it without authorisation and as far as I'm aware, no one has that authorisation in the UK to date. Technically, it's not even legal to give your pet CBD unless you have a prescription from a vet. So, it's an interesting space.

There are lots of reports, particularly if you look to the US, of people using CBD with their animals. I think the education within the veterinary system is still sort of fairly lacking. I know there are some vets who are happy to talk about CBD, but they tend to be in the minority.

Paul @ Herbotany Health

Well, the law currently in the UK states no, however anyone who benefits from CBD can make their own mind up.

Paul @ Naturecan

So, in the UK it has to be prescribed by a vet. In 22 countries, Naturecan has a pet range selling CBD. I give my pet my CBD daily, I've got a Dogue de Bordeaux Labrador Cross and they have notoriously bad hip joints.

So, it's something as preventative care that I give them, and we've got a full range of pet products, treats, oils, rubs, because you know, like the paws, where you don't think about balms for dogs, but it takes the inflammation out and heals it. We've got some great videos of how it's worked on our website.

Rowan @ Infinity CBD

They can. The law is very weird with this in the UK in the sense that the veterinary association has prevented selling or advised against selling CBD as pet products until further investigation has taken place.

Before this came in, we had loads of customers that were using it regularly with their dogs for epilepsy, or bad joints as they got older. You'd use a much smaller dose than you would for a person, but we know a lot of people that do. We just can't advise because of the current state of regulation.

Oren @ Kiara Naturals

I think that consumers do give CBD to their pets. I think there's quite a bit of research and definitely anecdotal experience from people that it's very beneficial.

I know that I used it for my parents' dog when he was still alive. It definitely works. I think there's much more room for error because they're more sensitive. And I think that recently in Europe, the regulations there are also starting to change and we're seeing more guidelines on CBD for pets. But definitely some pets benefit from it.

Jade @ Savage Cabbage

So, this is interesting because the Veterinary Medicines Directorate stopped the selling of products designed for the pet market back in 2018.

Now I'm aware, or I'm told, that some of the veterinary practices are look-ing into it, and you can get it somewhere, I think, for your pets. I don't feel qualified enough to answer the question. I do know that people buy it for their pets. And for those people, they tend to buy it in its most natural form.

So, they wouldn't buy a flavour, they wouldn't buy it in MCT, most generally in olive oil.

But when it comes to the amount of cannabinoids you're giving a pet, I wouldn't want to sort of jump into that partly because I don't know too much about it and it's something I've sort of steered away from.

How can I be sure CBD is safe?

Sophie & Jess @ Canax Life

I guess the best way for a consumer to ensure that CBD is safe, go and do your research. Are there any bad stories about CBD? Generally, you can't really find any if you go looking on the internet.

When you go to buy a CBD product, do they have their stability tests on their website so you can have a look?

Are they part of a governing body so that they follow the regulations? Is the labelling correct? Does it state the specific dose? What are the reviews like? Are they on the Novel Food list, everything like that? If they tick the boxes, I'd say it can be trusted.

But yeah, go and do your research and see if there's any bad stories that you can find and if someone's got a problem that you want to use it for, how did it help them?

Ben@ CBD Brothers

Just buy from someone that knows what they're doing.

Buy from a respectable company that's got a bit of provenance, a bit of longevity, and people that know what they're doing. Buy from people that you can speak to on the phone, or you can communicate with directly.

There's a reason we've got social media now, there's lots of benefits and whilst there's millions of curses, one of the best benefits is if you're dealing directly with a company you can go to these people directly on their Face-book page.

We've got people that work for us and use the products and will speak to people. If you have to go through a line that's then redirected to another number in another country, then I'd just leave them well alone.

You can come down to our farm and see us directly and see what we're up to, and there's not a lot of companies that are like that. So that's quite a good thing for me to say because that gives our company more kudos than everybody else. So that's it. Just check their provenance.

Matt @ Kloris CBD

I think the primary thing is to look at the brand that you are buying from.

Are they trustworthy? Are they presented in a credible way?

Is it very clear who is running that brand? Can you easily find out which company is behind the brand?

Who are the people behind that? Are they openly making available the certificates of analysis for all of their products?

And most importantly, are they up to date?

There should be a batch number on every product that you use. You should be able to find the certificate of analysis for that batch number, so if you're looking at a certificate of analysis on their website that is a couple of years old, that is a warning sign because the shelf life of all these products is going to be less than two years for a start.

It is very important to do a bit of research and just make sure that you are happy with the quality and consistency of that brand. If they've got reviews out there, are they reliable reviews? Are they trustworthy?

There's been a fairly prominent brand who have had an Advertising Standards Authority ruling against them. It turns out that all of their reviews and rewards they were claiming were circular, in that they'd all been paid for, and were all referencing the other reviews that they'd also paid for, so they had a cease and desist placed against them.

Paul @ Herbotany Health

My initial thought would be to log onto the Association for the Cannabinoid Industry webpage and purchase products from one of their member companies. Failing that, I would suggest that you only buy products from the current public list from the FSA.

Paul @ Naturecan

Hopefully, the Novel Food applications list will lead Trading Standards to take companies not on the list, off the shelves which will allow the consumer to have a bit more confidence.

What I would say at the moment is the consumer does need to be checking for Certificates of Authenticity and safety measures that people have on the websites or in the shops.

It's not even just some of the big shops that have recently been raided and had products taken off the shelves as well.

So, it isn't backstreet shops we're talking about. This is High Street. So, my big one is research. If you're putting anything in your body, make sure that they've had it tested and everything else before you buy.

Rowan @ Infinity CBD

So, you're going to get a lot of keywords around lab reports and where it's come from to make their products. Ultimately, these are things that should be standard, so therefore if you look for a product and check that it's on the FSA's Novel Food list, that will confirm that at the very least they've had to submit those things.

But ultimately that doesn't necessarily hold them to account to still do those things when they're selling them and it's a very saturated market.

So, my best advice is to look at the reviews but try for word of mouth and keep in mind to take reviews with a pinch of salt whilst reading through Facebook pages.

Don't just trust Trust Pilot and stuff like that, really look at that side of things to take people's personal experiences with the brand, going back beyond the last couple of months to see if there's someone using it longer term which is generally an indicator of something that is reputable.

Lab reports and stuff like that will help you work out the dose and make sure you are getting what you're paying for, but I've also seen plenty of things in the CBD industry where people are photoshopping these things. So, word of mouth is definitely the best way to kind of get your peace of mind for safety for sure.

Oren @ Kiara Naturals

I think CBD has been established by now as a pretty safe molecule. I recommend though to always consult with your physician or your therapist, somebody who knows your medical background.

Generally speaking, CBD products are very safe.

That's why, in the UK, we're seeing an established Novel Food market and CBD products that are being sold for intake.

Therefore, we know that they are safe. The other side of this, is you have to make sure that you're buying from a brand or a manufacturer, which you trust.

We're still seeing irregularities in pesticides and CBD amounts and mycotoxins.

So, you really have to make sure that the provider that you're buying from is giving you the lab analysis and that you can match that analysis to the actual batch number on your product, it's not just some generic test they did, and that you can see that everything is in order. It is worthwhile educating yourself on that.

Jade @ Savage Cabbage

I think to buy from a reputable brand, do your research on the brand. Ask for a Certificate of Analysis so you can view what's in that formulation.

Is there anything there that causes you any concerns?

A company not willing to share a Certificate of Analysis is one that I would avoid. I think that also with the Novel Foods list, we have currently in play, those companies that are listed and registered are ones that are currently being viewed by the FSA.

So that's a point of contact for people to go to and check if that brand that I'm looking at is on that list. If so, well, they're under evaluation so that ticks a box. Moving forward, I think that the FSA will have some kind of accreditation mark which sort of fulfils that consumer confidence piece.

What should I avoid when buying CBD?

Sophie & Jess @ Canax Life

For me, it definitely would be the information on the labelling and the packaging of the product, because that tells you everything that's inside and it should be very specific. So, if that's not on the packaging, I wouldn't buy it.

Look at the website. Are there any bad reviews? Are they on Trust Pilot as well? Is the brand known to people? Is it trusted?

Do you know anyone that's bought from them?

Word of mouth is the best form of finding out if something works. So, I think the less you know about something, maybe it's a higher risk product and that's what you should avoid when buying a CBD product.

Ben@ CBD Brothers

Don't buy from garages. Please don't buy from garages that sell one shot CBD things. Don't buy from anyone or anywhere that feels like it's a quick fix, with flashy signs.

I would avoid buying from companies that you can't look into and check. Just don't buy from garages. It's so infuriating.

Matt @ Kloris CBD

I would certainly avoid any products that are making explicit claims to cure or heal anything.

No brand in the CBD space should be doing that. If brands are outwardly doing that, it's not a great sign.

It suggests that they're more in this space for the money and you're not going to be getting the quality of end-product that you really expect.

At the end of the day, I would also be wary of products that are really cheap because they're really cheap for a reason. Good quality ingredients are expensive.

So, if you are finding it in a petrol station and it's five pounds on the counter in a clear plastic bottle, then this is not a great sign. It needs to be treated with care.

For example, you don't want to be storing it in plastic, particularly if it's an oil based product, because you will get leeching in there.

You don't wanna be storing it in clear bottles either, because the one thing that will break CBD down really quickly is sunlight, and particularly UV. So it needs to be in dark glass to store it properly. So, look for those things that show what this brand is paying attention to, the quality of the product.

Paul @ Herbotany Health

In my opinion, it's that the product is legal in this country. So, Broad Spectrum CBD as opposed to Full Spectrum, which is illegal because of the THC levels.

And secondly, I would always recommend that consumers buy natural CBD products rather than synthetic.

Paul @ Naturecan

For me, it would be judging the product just on the price. If you buy for price alone in the CBD market, you are not going to get the best quality product. A lot goes into making a finished product of CBD.

For example, our products are tested a minimum of six times from the start of the process, with the hemp, right the way through to a finished CBD product.

There's a certain expense that comes with it, but also a reassurance that the product is exactly what it says on that label, and free from pesticides, heavy metals, microbials, anything like that. So that would be my biggest advice.

Rowan @ Infinity CBD

It's very easy to get caught up in all the marketing spiel around different products. Ultimately, if you're looking to see if CBD is going to work for you for whatever reason, no matter who you go with, your best option is going to be with drops.

Just try the most effective absorption rate to get it into your system.

It's very easy to get distracted with gummies and chocolates for example, but if you want to make sure that it works for you before going into these other things, there's no better method in my opinion, than using drops, sublingually, and just stick to it for a week consistently.

Over the four years we've been in business, that's kind of been the most consistent way to find something that works, and a lot of customers fall off using CBD because they're trying different things each day and they're not seeing it help. Consistency with drops is definitely the best thing to stick to.

Oren @ Kiara Naturals

You should always buy from trustworthy established brands. If you're in the UK, they should be on the Novel Food list with the FSA.

Not to say that those who are not, are not good. It's just some form of screening.

You should make sure that they provide all the right analysis. And I always find that a money back guarantee for any period of time is a real value of trust that you can say, okay, this is not what I was looking for, take it back, give me back my money for whatever reason. So, don't buy from anybody who doesn't do all that.

Jade @ Savage Cabbage

Don't be guided by price. You know, there's a company out there that sells it for maybe five, six pounds a bottle.

How they're achieving that, I'm not quite sure. Are the contents going to be good quality?

Do your research and sort of look into what brands have been around. Speak to friends, ask questions but ultimately it is down to consumer choice. Everyone can put a pretty box and a fantastic design together, but actually it's more important what's inside that bottle and where it comes from.

What's its traceability? Where is the hemp grown? Where is all of this originating from?

And, you know, my personal preference is to look for a whole plant product or a Full Spectrum product.

I'm not a huge fan of Isolate, but that's just me and I believe in consumer choice. So, ask questions. We have a service for people where people can contact us and we'll give guidance and if you don't want to buy from us, that's fine, but we're still happy to help you.

Why is there so little clinical proof that CBD works?

Sophie & Jess @ Canax Life

Because it's such a new product, there's still so much unknown about it really and pharmaceutical companies are the only people that can do these huge clinical trials that cost millions of pounds.

There are smaller trials where it's used to explore things like neuropathy, after chemotherapy, anxiety, sleep. But for a big clinical trial, it's just too expensive. So, it's maybe not in their best interest at the moment to do it.

Ben@ CBD Brothers

There is tons of proof that cannabinoids work. It's one of the oldest studied plants. It was used by the ancient Egyptians to the Mesopotamians.

There's loads of proof.

What we've got is a specific compound that is being picked out and used but we've got millions of other things to do with cannabinoids that say that it helps, it works for these conditions. We've got anecdotal evidence, we've got recorded evidence, we've got peer reviewed evidence, we've got all of this evidence.

We know it works. It's just that the isolated compound of CBD hasn't been in the mainstream long enough for it to be studied. The research that was done in Israel when the cannabinoid system was studied proved that it had beneficial effects.

We can't have a system that's specifically targeted towards working with cannabinoids and then say, well, we've got no evidence.

The evidence is in your body, it's in your organs, it's in your skin, it's every-where that you need it to be. So, I don't agree that there is little evidence CBD works.

Matt @ Kloris CBD

A large part of this is due to the fact that for many, many years not only CBD, but all of the components of the cannabis plant were effectively prohibited so it was very hard to study the plant in any meaningful way.

That meant that actually studying it was very difficult to do because even if you wanted to do that at a research level, at a university, it was going to be very difficult to get funding for it and therefore that makes any sort of bulk of in-depth study really difficult.

What we're starting to see now is that it's rapidly changing because the market is there, it has opened up, it is now legal, so the research side is rapidly catching up. But like all of these things it takes time. It takes years and years of effort and peer review and research to really dig into this.

Even the endocannabinoid system itself wasn't seriously studied or discovered until the nineties. In terms of when you look at it compared to other medical compounds, it's far behind in terms of just the period of time people have had to research it.

Also, where CBD and cannabis as a whole fall into this interesting area of modern medicine and modern research, which is very much focused on single compound solutions, there's a very strong argument that you can't really look at cannabis and CBD in that same lens.

They are partnered, they work best when they're more in their natural setting where you're talking about hundreds and hundreds of different compounds and that doesn't very easily fit into modern healthcare models.

Paul @ Herbotany Health

I think that's purely because of the lack of trials by medical institutions throughout the world.

You could argue maybe that for the large drug companies it's not in their interest. But would I suggest that? I don't think so.

You only need to read some of our reviews on our site to see the benefits that our customers have from consuming our products or using our salves and topicals, to know that there is actually within the industry a fair bit of data to suggest that our products are beneficial.

Paul @ Naturecan

This is due to basically the prohibition of CBD for so many years, and it's only now starting to be researched. The other thing is who's going to pay for this research? That's what it always sort of comes down to and for me, it has to be the brands like ourselves.

We've been conducting several studies at John Moore's University in Liverpool, where the human studies have been on THC build-up, pain, double blind placebo, on how it affects anxiety, and everything else.

We've been running these studies for the last two years, we're involved in various different ones as well, but that's the only way that this is going to happen, is that the brands who are pushing this market have got to invest in it.

It's not going to come from a Government level. It has to be us and we're doing our bit.

Rowan @ Infinity CBD

I think it's a strange one because you'd think with all the different countries being ahead of us, there would be more funding behind it, but even when you're looking at America with the Farm Bill that passed within the last 24 months, I believe, it's only now that federally in the States, they're starting to put the real funding behind looking into CBD versus THC, which has kind of been the front runner in terms of research funding.

In the UK, just because studies come out elsewhere doesn't mean that you are able to present that to your customers here in the UK, because you need to have certain levels of accreditation.

The good news is that it is going that way.

Aberystwyth University is currently developing a Welsh CBD strain of cannabis and there's lots of other studies and trials going on throughout the UK at the moment. But frustratingly, it is somewhat limited at the moment, mainly on animal trials and reflective human feedback.

Oren @ Kiara Naturals

There is actually quite a bit of clinical evidence that CBD works, especially considering how young this molecule is in popular demand and popular use.

I mean, there's research on it coming out from the eighties in different clinics worldwide. I think what's really missing is peer reviewed placebo and double blind trials, that are more in the pharmaceutical realm because clinical studies and clinical research has been going on for four decades and it's been very promising and shown to be very safe.

What the pharmaceutical and regulatory bodies are looking for is clinical trials with placebo and toxicity studies, things which have not been done because really, it's a very new molecule.

Jade @ Savage Cabbage

I think because of the legislation on cannabis, it's prevented so much research for so many years and it's a huge problem.

However I think now there's been some changes in research licences and more have been applied for, so we will start to see more in the future.

It's just unfortunate that because of prohibition we've all been kind of hamstrung in how to access bits and pieces. We're starting to see more and more research being undertaken, which is encouraging.

But I think ultimately, it's just been down to the fact that it's been difficult to study a molecule that was legally restricted.

When buying CBD, how do I know I'm not being ripped off?

Sophie & Jess @ Canax Life

That's a hard one, isn't it. Because unless you take the product home and you have the machinery to check what's actually inside it, you don't know what you're buying, and it is about trusting that product.

So, to lower that risk of purchase, the more you can find out about that company, the better.

I think you don't want to be ripped off. Money's important, especially at the moment, people want something that works. They're looking for an end goal and with all our products, there is an end goal to help and that's what we get across all the time to people.

It's like anything, isn't it. Who knows when they're buying something, if it's going to work or not? But we hope that the fact that we are there to support you on your journey of trying CBD, you'll know you're not being ripped off.

So that's what I would say, I'd buy from CBD brand, where there's a story and real people behind it.

Ben@ CBD Brothers

By not buying from a garage, or companies that don't have a reputation. By avoiding anyone that hasn't been around longer than at least five years.

I'm not saying those that haven't been around longer than five years haven't done it properly, but you should have a little bit of evidence. Just don't buy from garages.

Matt @ Kloris CBD

I think the key if you're looking for a particular strength product is to ask for the Certificate of Analysis for that product to make sure it's matching up to what you are buying.

Make sure the batch numbers match, make sure the strength is what you were expecting it to be and ask yourself if it's a trustworthy brand that you're buying from. Do you have confidence in it? Have you heard of them? Have you seen people talking positively about that brand? Do they have all the elements you would look for in terms of credibility? Can you easily identify who is behind that brand?

If you're buying it online, I would look for simple triggers. Do they have a phone number, physical address, and actual legal name that you can identify on their website?

If they're trying to hide those things, I would be very wary. But that goes for online purchasing in general, but if they aren't willing to sort of explicitly say who they are behind that brand, I would steer well clear.

Paul @ Herbotany Health

Well, that's a very simple question. Buy from a reputable company who's a member of the ACI (Association for the Cannabinoid Industry).

Paul @ Naturecan

You want to check for testing, you want to check for reviews, that's the world that we live in now. If you've got a bad product, the consumer is going to shout about it. Reviews are something that we're always keen on. Customers giving honest feedback is always great to hear.

If you read our reviews, they're from impassioned people that have been helped by CBD. If you read some of the other reviews on some other sites, they're not quite to the same level but there are other good CBD sites with good reviews as well. So that would be the thing for me, go for peer to peer reviews.

These are the people that are buying the products and know what the service is like.

Rowan @ Infinity CBD

I think nowadays the price has settled quite a lot. And really there's probably only certain parameters that the price should be within for certain strengths.

At first, it was all over the place. It was very hard to tell because one product would be £30 and an identical copy £100. Now, I don't think that's so much of an issue.

Trust your sources when you're looking into reviews and compare a few different brands. A quick look on Reddit for example, will give you plenty of answers about the top five to ten brands in the UK.

Any of those are pretty good, at least they're a good indicator of where the price point should be and I think if you're paying any more than, say £40 for 1000mg you're probably paying more than you need to, so look at other brands and see where they're positioned, if you've found someone you haven't heard about before.

Orun @ Kiara Naturals

First of all, you should look around and see the prices, and if you're buying something that's unusually expensive, you're probably being ripped off. The market is very competitive and there's a lot of options so as a consumer, you should take advantage of that.

You should also look at the concentration of CBD oil that you're buying. You can calculate that according to milligrams. It's quite easy. You say, okay, this has 500mg of CBD, there's 200 drops inside, you divide 500 by 200 and you know how many milligrams you have in every bottle.

You can do this for several different products and that figure you get in the end is the amount that you're paying per milligram. If you see one that's exceptionally high, you're probably getting ripped off. You do and should need to combine this with actually seeing that it's a trustworthy brand.

You don't want to just go for the cheapest thing out there. You want to make sure that they have their analysis in place, that you know who's behind the brand, that they're trustworthy. But they have their certificates and that you don't want to get ripped off, but you don't want to get a terrible, unhealthy product, which is much worse, I think.

Jade @ Savage Cabbage

I think that you need to look at the contents of the bottle. You need to look at what's in there.

Are we looking at a CBD isolate? Are we looking at a whole plant? Are there any other active components in there?

A bit like Ronseal, is it going to do what it says on the tin?

Contact the companies directly for information, look at their websites. It's all there to instil consumer confidence. It's important for people to understand that they might not get an immediate response from CBD.

They may not have an immediate kind of, you know, 'oh, I felt that', or 'I've noticed something'. So, perseverance and patience are also key to trying a brand, giving it a full month, reviewing that, reflecting on that and making your own mind up from there.

What happens if I exceed the daily recommended dose?

Sophie & Jess @ Canax Life

Nothing major will happen. If you take excessive amounts, especially on an empty stomach, you may find you feel a little bit sick or you have an upset tummy which could lead to diarrhoea. Nothing life-threatening at all. So no, nothing major will happen if you take in excess of the recommended amount.

Ben@ CBD Brothers

You might get a bad stomach and spend a couple of hours on the toilet or something like that. You might feel a bit sick. So definitely stick to the recommended dose as decreed by the FSA.

Matt @ Kloris CBD

In the UK, the recommended dose currently under the FSA rules is 70 milligrams of ingested CBD per day. Now in other countries, it's much, much higher, going up to a 1,000mg.

So arguably, most people are not gonna find ill effects if they accidentally consume more, particularly if it's a high quality product and you haven't got any of the other sort of cannabinoids in there, like THC for example, which are things where you would tend to see a negative effect if you consume them in excess or in any quantity depending on the person.

In general, CBD is considered exceptionally safe. We have these guidelines in place out of an abundance of caution whilst there's still more research being done.

Paul @ Herbotany Health

As a responsible business owner and CBD user, I would always suggest that any of our customers stick within the 70mg recommended maximum dose per day, certainly for the time being.

Personally, I do not have a problem with exceeding that dose, certainly on occasions. But I would certainly not suggest that any of our customers do so until there's more data to suggest otherwise.

Paul @ Naturecan

In the UK, it's 70mg per day. In Australia it's 150mg and in another country it has been set at 200mg.

So, this is something that the research has to examine. I take more than 70 milligrams a day because I know how my endocannabinoid system works and it needs a heavier dose at the end of the day to help me sleep and everything else.

Research has to go into this and as I've said before there has been research done with a 2000 milligram daily intake. So there's big discrepancies with this, we've got a higher number through ethics at the John Moore University as well, because we feel that 70mg is definitely at the lower end of what it will be soon.

So that would be my opinion on it and it should be a little bit higher, but it's strictly 70mg at the moment from the FSA.

Rowan @ Infinity CBD

Some people are quite sensitive to CBD so in lower dosages than others, they'll already feel kind of more of an onset, whereas others won't even notice.

I've certainly made mistakes where I've accidentally taken a lot more than I intended to and for me I've just got really drowsy. Whereas others, from whom we've had feedback, who have taken too much, some have issues like feeling a bit more anxious.

But I do wonder how much of that is them being anxious about what will happen, rather than what does happen. A prime example being our chocolate bars, when someone thinks they can eat the whole bar in one go, instead of two squares and then miss the end of a film they're watching!

Oren @ Kiara Naturals

In my experience, nothing. The daily recommended dose is 70mg for an average adult, which is calculated from 75 kgs of body weight. We've seen both personally and in our private practices and with our customers, that it's very hard to overdose on CBD if it's even possible.

All the research that goes out on CBD from the in-lab testing on animals, all the way to human testing, they test enormous amounts of CBD. I'm talking up to a gram a day, that's a thousand milligrams a day and we're seeing very little undesired effects, if at all.

There was one study that was blown up into this massive case of liver toxicity, but it was inadequately done, and it's been discarded since. Until now, I can't say that I know of anything bad that happens. I've only seen positive effects.

Jade @ Savage Cabbage

So, the recommended daily allowance currently from the FSA is 70mg but that's just a recommendation. So I'm somebody who would probably consume around 140-ish mg per day. I'm not aware of anybody that has ever had any negative side effects from taking more than 70mg per day.

Again, it's a recommendation, not a rule. But again, there's going to be some emerging evidence which is coming out with regards to the isolate component, and I believe in my heart that the recommended daily allowance for an isolate may perhaps change.

Who knows. But ultimately, it's there. Use it and if you've taken more than your recommended daily allowance, I don't foresee any problems. But I'm going to caveat that with, I'm not a scientist and I'm not a doctor so it's down to the individual. And if you've got some concerns, then speak to your primary care practitioner.

Why is CBD currently so expensive?

Sophie & Jess @ Canax Life

I think it's expensive because it's expensive to produce. The process involved in production is expensive. All the safety controls and testing are expensive and also most CBD is imported, we get ours from Oregon, so being from the US, it's obviously the expense of bringing it into the country as well.

Ben@ CBD Brothers

I think you have to look at the process that goes into making CBD products.

I'm very conscious that some of our extracts have been some of the most expensive on the market for quite a long period of time, but that's very specific to a specific extract that we put a lot of care and attention into the growing process.

If you look at what we've been publishing on our Facebook page up until now, you'll see that the process we're going through is extensive. We're not just chucking 20 million seeds in a 10 acre field and harvesting it, squashing it, and doing the bare minimum to look after it.

We're growing very selective plants. We're doing a lot of strain development. We're doing a lot of care and management. We do a lot to help make sure that the end product is the absolute best it can be for the consumer.

Now, I could produce CBD that would cost next to nothing and in fact some of our extracts are some of the cheapest on the market. So, we've got both ends of the spectrum. But my preferred extract, our Indica extract is the one that we have the best reputation with because quite frankly, it is the best that's on the market because of the amount of care and attention,

We're completely transparent about the process. You can see every aspect from the clones we make, to the planting and the soils. We don't use pesticides; we use natural predators. Now we get through millions and millions of natural predators every growing season. Now those aren't cheap to come by and we have to factor in all these things.

What you get is the choice of whether you want to get something that's been mass produced and chucked out quickly, or if you want to get something that's been cared for and maintained in a good way.

There's a lot of energy that you can put into these things and we've always found by taking the handcrafted route, by taking a slower route, we end up with a better extract and product for the consumer.

Matt @ Kloris CBD

I think there's a number of factors involved and there's still a lot of development going on within the industry. You have to invest quite heavily in the infrastructure behind growing and then harvesting CBD, particularly if it's been done in sustainable and high quality ways.

So, you need things like organic agriculture, which is not cheap to do and you need high quality extraction methods, which require very expensive equipment.

It's not something that is done well at industrial scale yet, so the emphasis is on small scale producers doing things in an extremely high quality way.

Things like organic farming are very important with hemp cultivation because it will absorb pretty much anything that is in the soil or sprayed on it, so you need to take great care when you are growing those plants and then extracting the CBD.

There is a lot of care and attention needed throughout the supply chain and it's a very new area still. CBD has only been in the market for four or five years. So, you're still seeing early investment in the UK.

Also, you can't grow hemp for CBD extraction in the UK so that means everything has to be imported and that's always got a whole lot more difficult in recent years as well.

There are a lot of barriers to trade in the UK. Hopefully that will change because it's frankly ludicrous that you can't grow hemp for extraction in the UK. It's missing out a huge part of the value chain that would be enormously beneficial to the UK industry, to UK farming, even to the UK environment because hemp is such a brilliant biomediator and carbon store. But that's another topic!

Paul @ Herbotany Health

I think any responsibly sourced and manufactured product is expensive for a reason. I don't think I need to say any more than that. It's the ingredients, the way it's made, the checks that are done, and becoming part of a regulated industry is also a huge investment for any responsible company in the CBD field.

Paul @ Naturecan

I think this is down to the process that you go through. I can actually buy CBD in Oregon cheaper than we can make it.

I think the price of raw CBD has come down slightly over the last year or two, but other prices have increased around it, like shipping, so it's been a little bit of a balance from a finished product perspective. Testing is expensive, $300-$600 a time and every single batch is being tested six times along the process.

We don't just stick a bit of CBD oil in with a bit of cheap MCT, we use organic MCT, and our CBD comes from organic hemp flour and that is a lot more expensive.

Note: MCT (Medium Chain Triglyceride) oil is fat-based and rich in caproic acid, caprylic acid, capric acid and lauric acid. MCT oil is used as a carrier for CBD because it helps to increase bioavailability.

Rowan @ Infinity CBD

I think it's a weird one because you've got two sides of the industry. You've got people who are really into CBD already fully aware of it, and therefore understand what the price points are in accessing the raw ingredients.

Then you've got the other side that are either trying to profit from it greatly and putting their prices up really high, or businesses that are just trying to remain competitive. But as with any business there are high overheads and Covid hasn't helped with the supply chain issues.

We're very lucky that we've not had any impact on the CBD coming into the country for us because we work with someone in the UK that already has it, whereas a lot of companies don't have that benefit.

So, when there's delays with transport, when there's more import charges on top, or quite a lot of people are still getting seizures at the border, even though they are legal.

You've got to build that into your cost basis. So unfortunately, there's still associated costs and especially when you've got smaller companies that have staff to pay, it's not as cheap and easy as it is when you're mixing it at home. So, yes, it's a lot cheaper than it was, but it still has a little way to go.

Oren @ Kiara Naturals

Well, first of all, it's getting less and less expensive.

The first reason it's so expensive is this is still a very concentrated matter coming from a plant. People still need to grow this and the product that consumers are holding at the end has had hundreds, if not thousands of people involved in its manufacturing.

Second, it's highly regulated and yet not regulated enough to give freedom to the industry. So, everything in the CBD industry is more expensive. If you want to move products from one area to the other, it's more expensive. If you want to sell it online, it's more expensive.

These are the two main drivers.

But you have to remember that in a 30% ten ml bottle of CBD, you could have up to 4kg's of CBD plant matter extracted into that.

So, this is a highly concentrated product. Hemp is a complicated plant to grow and I believe that for the benefit when correctly used, that the products are already at a very fair price.

Jade @ Savage Cabbage

I think it varies. I mean there are some brands out there which are really, really expensive and I really question why. But if we look at say, the Charlotte's Web Origin in a 100ml bottle, you are looking at about £240.

Now, somebody would look at that and potentially go, 'holy moly', that's a lot of money.

But if you're looking at the cannabinoid content, you are looking at patented genetics. You are looking at a vertically integrated company with a value chain from seed through to shelf.

Every process is managed and tested 20 times before it moves onto its next process and the time and cost put into the development of the product is therefore reflected in that.

When we look at the Savage Cabbage range, that comes in at a lower cost, that's because I own it and I'm able to price it for people who may not be able to afford the Charlotte's Web range. Now, I could make more profit on that if I wanted to, but that doesn't sit right with my moral compass.

Are the more expensive CBD brands better?

Sophie & Jess @ Canax Life

You don't know what goes on behind the scenes. So, the production of CBD itself is very costly and buying it in raw material form is expensive. You don't know how much packaging costs are behind the scenes of a brand.

So, when it comes to deciding on a retail price for a product, all of that has to be considered. And just because one product is more expensive doesn't mean it's better or it's going to work better. There might just be reasons for why that's more expensive. So, do your homework, go on the websites, read the reviews, and then hopefully come to a decision that way.

Ben@ CBD Brothers

We know the provenance of everything; where it's come from and we can monitor it all the way through the process. So yes, I believe that they're better because I believe they have a higher cannabinoid content. I believe that there's a lot more attention that goes into making them.

Paul @ Herbotany Health

Yes. Our own brand is certainly at the higher end of the pricing spectrum. There are reasons for that, which I've already explained. And you get what you pay for.

Paul @ Naturecan

I'd say that for the more expensive brands, because they're testing, because they're buying the highest quality ingredients, then definitely.

But there are some that are just marketing a cheaper product. There's no doubt in my mind, definitely more in the States than over in Europe, I'd say. But certainly, in the UK I know of a few products that are the same product that somebody sells for a third of the price, exactly the same product from the same facility with a different label on it.

I think that's part of the research that you've got to do into these brands as well. Check out where the product's coming from.

Rowan @ Infinity CBD

Sometimes yes, sometimes no.

I think beforehand a lot of the more expensive brands were more discernible from the others and there are arguments to be made that if you have an extract that was grown, say in America with a broader range of species, and strains of cannabis that have more terpenes in, then actually there is a benefit to paying more.

Oren @ Kiara Naturals

Well, they're not necessarily better, but more expensive brands can afford to do more quality assurance. They can afford to be more selective with the raw ingredients, which is not always the case.

Sometimes brands simply, for the sake of being expensive and making more money, will be expensive. But as a consumer, you can check that and ask for their certifications.

You can read about their story, their lab analysis and so on. You can check why their product is so expensive.

So, are they necessarily better? No, but I can tell you that it is very hard to make a high quality product at a cheap price.

Jade @ Savage Cabbage

I wouldn't say they were better. Uniquely different, perhaps. I mean, Charlotte's Web's original project formula is the gold standard of CBD in this industry, and that's undeniable.

And you know, I am very much a strong believer in that. I don't know how people come up with some of their prices.

You know, you could go to a very expensive shop that's based in London, and you could go and spend £800 on a product, which is crazy and really ridiculous. They're probably not selling that many bottles at that price.

If you look at what the general cost is, it falls to a range which is around £50 to £60 pounds. If you're looking at a 30mg bottle of a middle strength oil, anything below that I would sort of look at a little more closely.

How do I identify good quality CBD?

Sophie & Jess @ Canax Life

I think there's quite a few different ways. Our first call would be to look at the reviews. We have put our application into the Food Standards Agency, with a certificate of analysis, which is on our website showing our lab results.

Third party lab test results, that's always a good one

Always look at the product to see if it displays the amount of CBD in it or not. That's definitely a must.

Make sure that it contains less than 0.2% of THC.

Make sure that the company's not making any ridiculous medical claims.

Make sure that they're being genuine of what they're saying. I think a good one is if they're being environmentally friendly.

I'd also look at organic as well. I always think that's quite a good one, we source our CBDs from an organic farm.

Ben@ CBD Brothers

I'd look at the company, look at their reputation. Check the reviews. Check with other people and your peers.

Just look into it a little bit. We've been very open. We have good Facebook engagement. We've always had good social media engagement and we've got that for a reason, because we're happy to talk about what we're doing.

We know what we're talking about, and they're the guys you need to speak to; the guys that are happy to speak to you, the guys that know what they're doing and have got the history and longevity in the business, and have been around the block.

Matt @ Kloris CBD

I think the primary things are the usual things that you would look at if you were trying to identify a high quality brand. Is that brand presenting trust-worthiness?

Are they available in the kind of places that you would expect a high quality brand to be?

Have they got an established background with CBD in particular?

All brands should be testing their products. The only way you can make sure that the ultimate strength and purity of the product is what they say it is, is to have a third party laboratory test done on it.

Brands should be presenting that for their products and for each batch, very clearly on their website. They should make that information freely available.

Those certificates should be very clear and show exactly what is in that product. They should show not only the CBD concentration, but all the other major cannabinoids in there, so you can make sure that it doesn't have things like THC or CBN which are the two psychotropic cannabinoids that also happen to be illegal in the UK.

So that kind of information should be very clearly available. It should be from a government accredited laboratory as well, of which there are a few now in the UK that are very used to dealing with cannabis. And if you can't access that basic information, that should be a key warning sign for you.

Paul @ Herbotany Health

I would suggest using a member of the ACI platform. And you couldn't get a better start than Herbotony Health.

Paul @ Naturecan

I'd say it's checking out their testing on their website for Certificates of Application and paperwork. Peer-to-peer reviews.

They're the ones that just cannot lie. If there's no review site on them, then they don't want people talking about their brand. Check the review sites out and see what the worst part of it is as well.

Check the good reviews but check the bad ones as well and see what the issue is and if it's not a product quality issue.

Some people just have had a disaster on delivery or anything like that, it happens to everybody in every sort of business, but as long as it's not quality related issues, that's what you should go with.

Rowan @ Infinity CBD

I think once you've established that there's a brand you've heard from word of mouth or you've got reviews backing up the kind of quality, that's when you can step into the lab reports, which should be available.

If it's a reputable brand, it's at that point that the first thing you do is check the CBD content is what they've said it would be. Beyond that, it's looking into the other cannabinoids.

For example, you can have someone selling broad spectrum CBD, because it has CBG and CBN in it, which does define it as broad spectrum, but it might have nothing else.

You want to look at all the other cannabinoids and flavonoids and see the richness in that side of it, because adding CBG and CBN is great, but you want as much of the original cannabinoids found in the extract as possible.

That's a mark of a good quality.

Oren @ Kiara Naturals

You should look for their brand story. Who is behind the brand? Are the people behind the brand visible? Are they putting themselves out there?

This is true now for consumerism in general. Does the company stand for the values that you stand for? Do they recycle? Are they plastic neutral? Are they bioorganic?

These are very high signs of quality. Then specific for the CBD world, you should be asking for lab analysis for every product.

Those products should match batch numbers to the lab analysis. You should be able to trace your product all the way to that result, and that brand that you are buying from should have on their website some way of educating yourself on how to read those analyses.

I would say that the key three things you want to make sure of are;

First of all, pesticides. This is an agricultural product. A lot of people use pesticides that you don't want.

Second would be heavy metals. That's again an agricultural product, there are heavy metals in the earth which you don't want.

And last is the cannabinoids. Within the products you want to take, make sure you're getting what you're paying for.

Jade @ Savage Cabbage

I think I can only speak from my own experience. What I would answer with is I have never spent money on marketing, and yet we have a community that covers 44 countries, and that's all been through word of mouth.

So that tells me that we're doing something correctly and that people have got confidence in what we do and how we do it because they keep coming back to us.

I think that storytelling, sharing experiences, and having a face and a personality attached to a brand is very important.

There are companies out there which will stick a pretty label on a bottle and put it on a shelf and hope that it sells.

But where's the personality and how can customers connect if they know nothing about the brand?

I've told my story so many times I wonder if people are bored, but I hope it helps people relate and understand why I am doing this, why I'm concerned and why I care. I think it helps with the element of trust with consumer products.

What form of taking CBD delivers the most benefit?

Sophie & Jess @ Canax Life

Taking CBD in any form is beneficial. However, if you take it sublingually, it'll go through your mucus membrane, which is the quickest way for the CBD to get into your system.

So, for example, our gummies are coated in oil and when you take a gummy that will go through your mucus membrane and then the rest of the gummy will go through your digestive tracts which will have residue CBD on it, and that will be longer lasting.

It depends how quick you want to get it into your system really. The quickest way is sublingual and then longer lasting through your digestive system with an edible.

Ben@ CBD Brothers

I think suppositories provide the most benefit to people that are taking CBD or cannabinoid products.

We don't do a suppository because it's very difficult to get that done and British people have a thing for (not) sticking things up our bum which is kind of understandable. It's not a method that I like to use.

However there's a reason they do this, because you've got a higher absorption rate in the canal of your rectum allowing the medicine to pass through.

There are few people in the industry that will say, 'oh no, it doesn't work', it's nonsense. It does work. Time and time again you can see that it works. We always get the best and see the best results with people who use pessaries or suppositories.

However, after that, I'm old school with droppers and oils and things like that. But if I've got a mark on my arm or something like that, then I'll apply a topical because the closer you can get it, the better it's going to start working.

So, suppositories first. But also, dropper bottles are good.

Matt @ Kloris CBD

I think it really depends on what you're looking to get from it. What's the most convenient method for you, but also what are you looking to get from that product?

If you are looking for help with aches and pains and joint aches, things like that, you'll probably find things like a topical balm are a better approach for you because they're acting directly to the specific local area and they're really easy to apply.

You can use them as often as you need.

Whereas if you were taking CBD systemically, via oil drops is probably the most common route.

But also, I find probably the biggest component for most people is, well, what's the convenient route for you?

A lot of people have been using oil drops because that's been the first most accessible method of getting hold of the CBD for a long time. That's where it really first became available, so people are used to that.

They can control their dosing with that, take as much or as little as they like and when they need it, but for some people it's just convenient.

We sell a lot of CBD patches now, which use transdermal absorption technology. So, it's getting into the bloodstream.

There's evidence there to suggest that it's getting into the bloodstream much more efficiently than if you're taking it orally even, under the tongue. And they're very, very convenient for a lot of people because they're slow release and you can forget about it.

It really depends on what you're looking for, how it fits into your lifestyle as well and whether you want to be taking it on a regular, continual basis, Or you're just looking to have assistance from it every now and again.

Paul @ Herbotany Health

I think it's a fairly widely known fact that any ingestible, particularly tinctures or capsules are probably the best ways to take CBD. I personally love our capsules.

We have a ground-breaking technology, which actually makes the bio-availability of our capsules at least 2-3 times more effective than any of our competitors.

Paul @ Naturecan

This is a bit of a 'horses for courses', so for me, I love sublingually because it hits me straight away. I know people that vape CBD because they're in a lot of pain, like fibromyalgia sufferers, things like that where there's not a go-to pain relief.

So, it's fast acting. The fastest acting way is vaping it. It goes straight in.

Sublingually you feel something straight away, but around 12 - 20 minutes before you feel it topically.

For some, if you've got a bad shoulder, I always recommend that you take oral CBD, but you also put a topical on there as well, because it has other ingredients that are going to help the inflammation. If you take the inflammation out of something, it's going to kill the pain.

Rowan @ Infinity CBD

I think the two most efficient methods would either be sublingual, holding it under your tongue, followed by swallowing, or vaping. But an option between the two to avoid the inhalation would naturally be the drops.

Personally, I accept that it's not for everyone due to the taste, but in terms of effectiveness and trying to make sure that you're taking a dose, where as much of it is being absorbed as possible, I think holding it under the tongue, for 60-90 seconds, followed by swallowing, is probably the best method.

Oren @ Kiara Naturals

Well, I would say that it really depends on what benefits you're trying to get, but definitely the most efficient way to take CBD is through vaping. When you vape CBD, I know it's controversial, but there's about 98% absorption going through the lungs directly into the bloodstream.

When you consume it sublingually or through ingestion, that goes down to between 6 to 12% and on the skin it's even less.

So really, the most effective way is vaping. But I find that the ingestible root is most effective for people who are trying to get health benefits from it for pain, anxiety, stress, because the absorption curve is much slower.

So instead of having this inhalation peak and then drop, you're going to have a slow and long-lasting curve, that is actually what you want.

Jade @ Savage Cabbage

What I would say is tinctures have the most immediate effect. Obviously, it absorbs straight into the body. Quite convenient. I am quite partial to the gummies. I do like the gummies. I've always got some gummies in my bag when I'm out and about doing things.

But obviously, you know, you've got to eat them, digest them, absorb them through your stomach acid. You're looking at about 40 minutes. So, bio-availability is really important. I would obviously just say that tinctures first and foremost are the most impactful delivery method.

Are all CBD products vegan friendly?

Sophie & Jess @ Canax Life

No. There's plenty of brands out there that aren't vegan friendly. For us, we wanted to be vegan friendly, and we wanted our whole product range to be vegan friendly, which has caused quite a few problems.

We wanted to bring a sugar free gummy out, but we really struggled to find a vegan friendly one. We did manage to eventually, so all our capsules and all our gummies are vegan friendly, because we wanted to involve everybody. But no, there are brands out there that aren't vegan friendly.

Ben@ CBD Brothers

Our capsules are vegan, the oil is vegan, everything we apply is vegan. Unless animals have been harmed in the making of the glass for the bottle it goes in, I don't understand how you would get a non-vegan CBD product, unless you're deliberately going out of your way to put something non-vegan in there, which is a bit of a silly thing to do.

I would check though to make sure it has a vegan mark because, don't take my word for it, some products might not be vegan friendly.

Matt @ Kloris CBD

Not necessarily. I mean, it would generally come down to what they are mixed with, so ultimately your CBD product is going to be combined with something. When we talk about CBD, we can be talking about two potentially different things.

CBD can exist in a relatively pure form. So, you're talking about CBD isolate here, which is a white crystal and powder generally in its normal form, and that's then mixed with a carrier oil, a food product or a topical product.

Then it's about the things that it's being mixed with, so in some products you might have beeswax, which is arguably not vegan depending on your point of view.

Really though it is all about the other things that it's combined with in that you've got broad spectrum CBD, which is arguably more premium and has other cannabinoids which comes in the form of, in its base form, a viscous oil.

This will need to be mixed with other things to make it into a state where you can either use it in a topical product or you can ingest it in some form. So generally, CBD is vegan safe, in its raw form, as it's coming from a plant but then you need to look at what the CBD is combined with to establish if it's vegan friendly.

Paul @ Herbotany Health

I can't vouch for all CBD products, but I'm pretty confident that Herbotany Health products are vegan friendly.

Paul @ Naturecan

Not all finished CBD products are vegan friendly.

We have a huge range of vegan products, but we've got a CBD protein that contains milk, so that one is not vegan.

One of the chocolates in our range isn't vegan. It's only suitable for vegetarians, obviously with the milk. I'd say probably 90% of our products are vegan.

Our soft gels are another that's an example of not being vegan, but we do a vegan capsule with the same milligram intake. It's something that we definitely prefer to offer, and we have a big gummy range that's vegan as well, but unfortunately not in all cases.

We have got Kosher certificates for our CBD and we're working on Halal now with our facility in Oregon.

We definitely want to make sure that CBD is open to everybody whatever your dietary requirements.

Rowan @ Infinity CBD

Definitely not, no. You'd like to think that most are, and they should be, because obviously it's a plant extract and it should just be added to a carrier oil mostly.

But when you're talking about a product being vegan friendly, it's more than that; it comes down to your labs and however the product is being made as well, just to make sure there's no contamination.

Going beyond that into the packaging, you have a lot of people setting up white label brands and they won't necessarily have their finger on every step of the way to make sure that there's no issues with pigmentation or having vegan issues in the packaging or the boxes or labels that they use, or other aspects of the bottles.

We found some shocking things that contain animal products along our way. So, it's definitely something that could be overlooked by others. It's worth tracking for sure.

Oren @ Kiara Naturals

Absolutely not. I would say that it really depends on what else is in the product. Some bees actually like hemp and I guess they would get damaged in their lifecycle. But CBD oils should be vegan friendly unless the carrier oil is made from some nasty stuff. We have a product, for example, a salve that has beeswax inside. Therefore, it's not vegan.

Jade @ Savage Cabbage

I can't see why they wouldn't be. I just suppose it depends on what the carrier oil is and where that comes from but ultimately, I don't see why they wouldn't be vegan. I think when it comes to the gummies, Charlotte's Web gummies are vegan. But yeah, with tinctures, unless I'm missing something glaringly obvious, I can't think why they wouldn't be vegan.

When is the best time to take my CBD?

Sophie & Jess @ Canax Life

We find, especially with our consumers, the best time for them is after dinner.

So maybe an hour or a couple of hours before, when you're winding down and you want to relax and get ready for a nice restful sleep.

However, some people do have their CBD in the mornings if they want to start the day off nice and calm. What we do suggest, is have it with food though, because like any supplement, if you have it on an empty stomach, it might make you feel a bit upset.

Maybe during the day as well, depending what's going on. But yeah, CBD is a funny one because it's not a written rule, it's different for everyone. So, for some people it might work in the morning, but most generally in the evening.

Ben@ CBD Brothers

I'm very much an hour before you go to bed person. However, if I was suffering from anxiety at 12 o'clock in the afternoon, I wouldn't then wait until the evening to take my CBD.

It depends on the condition and what you are needing support for. We get a lot of people wanting our Indicas for lack of sleep and insomnia and things like that, so in that case, I'd say take an hour before you go to bed.

People in pain, especially with the weather being as it is at the moment, they'll wake up feeling a bit iffy.

So again, I'd say take it immediately after you wake up, if you've got the option to do that, and wait for it to kick in and do its magic thing.

Matt @ Kloris CBD

That is very much an individual thing, so it will partly depend on what you are looking to get from the CBD.

If people are typically using it to help them sleep, then we generally advise that the main dose is taken shortly before bed. If you're using it for stress related reasons, then it's best to take CBD around that moment of peak need.

But a lot of people will take a daily maintenance dose treating it like a supplement, much like their vitamin supplements, where the most important thing is taking it when it fits into your schedule so you can build it in as part of your routine. So, if that's in the morning, then great. If that's at night for you, then that's totally fine.

I think what matters is that there is consistency and also how you are taking it. If you're taking it via oral drops or ingesting it, CBD is a fat soluble compound, you'd be best to be taking CBD when you are also having some other fats and ingesting them, because that will just help you get as much of it as possible into your system.

So, if you're going to be having it in the morning, then having it before breakfast and including some sort of fatty foods in your breakfast, you get that little bit extra from the CBD that you're taking.

Paul @ Herbotany Health

I think it depends on whether you are taking it regularly or if you are taking it on occasions because you feel anxious or to help you sleep.

If you are taking it regularly, I would suggest the same time of the day, preferably when you've eaten. But I have no opinion on whether you should take it in the morning or the evening.

All I would suggest is try ingesting it at a similar time each day if you are taking it regularly.

Paul @ Naturecan

Depending on what you're taking it for. Personally for me it's 15 minutes before bed, which is a perfect time for me to relax, turn the phone off, get the phone on charge, take my CBD, sort the last bits out, and go to bed.

For some people who are suffering with anxiety, which is a lot of people, they talk to us via reviews, they take it first thing in the morning.

I remember one review distinctly where they take it before they open their eyes in the morning. You know, it's the first thing that they do, so it's different for different people.

If you're training hard, like Andy, my business partner who trains in the gym for a couple of hours a day, lifts massive weights and everything else, his time is after exercise. So, he'll have a protein shake with some CBD to help recovery and then usually, before bed to help recovery during sleep. So, horses for courses.

Rowan @ Infinity CBD

Well, I guess it depends on the reason that you're taking it. For me, I find first thing in the morning and about an hour or so before bed is the best time for me to take my doses.

But that's when I'm mostly in need, is to get going and then to wind down. Whereas others will find that taking their dose in the middle of the day.

Other people will only use it ad hoc. So maybe it's an hour before they go to the gym or just as they finish a particular activity.

It's certainly one of the hardest things to establish as part of your routine, but also really important to be open to adapting it and to be fine. I believe it's what works for you.

Oren @ Kiara Naturals

I think it really depends on what you're trying to get the benefits for. If you're suffering from pain throughout the day, you should be taking it in the morning or throughout the day.

If it's more for anxiety and stress, again you can take it when you need it throughout the day. Some people have their anxiety more towards the evenings or the mornings where I suggest taking it just before you go to bed as well for sleep

If you are looking to improve your overall wellness. I would take it quite regularly throughout the day and keep that going for some time.

Jade @ Savage Cabbage

Well, I would argue that it very much depends on what you are looking for.

Through my research and readings, I'm not claiming that I know this to be absolute, but the lower amounts of cannabinoids you take, can be antagonistic. So, it can make you more energetic, more alert, and more focused.

If you then were to take a full 70 milligrams, that's going to be more calming, restful, and help you sort of settle down in preparations for bed.

It really depends on what you want to get from it.

What I do is bookend the day, currently I will start my day with 20 milligrams and then I have another 20 milligrams after lunch and then I load up with a good dollop an hour before bed. I get what I need from using my products like that.

How much CBD should I be taking?

Sophie & Jess @ Canax Life

We get this one quite often and it's hard to explain, but what we suggest to our consumers, as a baseline, we normally say about 0.25mg per pound in weight.

But what I would also suggest is it all depends on the consumer's metabolism, when they take it, how often they take it. Also, it depends what they're treating.

So, say if you're treating pain relief, we would always advise to have more. Also, if you've never taken CBD before, we would obviously explain to start off small because people are more sensitive than others.

So, we sometimes recommend for our gummies to take half a gummy to one gummy to start off with and then build up, and then they'll find their sweet spot.

Ben @ CBD Brothers

Well, you've obviously got to follow the recommended daily allowance that's outlined by the FSA. That's a very important thing to remember.

However, the best thing to do is try it and see how you get on with it.

For some people, there's no set marker. This is the kind of bonkers thing about it. Some people will need very little, some people will need a lot. So, you've got to really start off on a low level and work your way up. Which is why one of our favourite sayings is to start low and slow.

Take a couple of drops for five days, then build up, build up, build up until you find it works.

But if you get to a point when you're drinking a bottle and nothing's happening and it's not working, just stop taking it because you may need some guidance.

Matt @ Kloris CBD

What we advise, and this is following the guidelines of the Medical Cannabis Clinicians Society as well, is that it will vary from individual to individual.

So, the most important thing is to start low and build that dose up slowly over time.

We generally recommend starting with a dose of around five to 10mg, maintaining that dose for at least a week, evaluating how you feel at that point, and then slowly increasing that dose if you feel the need.

Different people respond in very different ways because it's about stimulating your body's endocannabinoid system. It's all about how deficient that system is in the first place and therefore how much stimulation it needs, but also how responsive your particular genetic makeup is to that stimulation.

We have customers who say they literally take one drop a day of our lowest strength 5% oil. It's absolutely fine. We have other customers who need far more of our strongest oil to get the same effect.

It's such an individual thing and so I always advise customers to start low, build up slowly, to work out the right dose for you.

Because if you go straight in and you start taking more than you need, you're going to secrete the CBD that you are not using at that point and wasting your money at that point. So it's much better to build up over time, adjust and really work out what is the sweet spot for you.

Paul @ Herbotany Health

Everyone's metabolism is different. We certainly won't suggest any of our customers take any more than the maximum approved dosage per day.

All of our Herbotony CBD products come with very clear instructions on what the maximum dosage per day is and also particularly on our tinctures, instructions for making sure you get a dose which you require rather than risking taking too much.

Paul @ Naturecan

At the start, this is probably the question our customer service team get asked the most - and it's all about titration.

You've got to make sure you start slow and low and build yourself up.

Find your level. If you immediately go for 250mg, way over the recommended daily dose, you don't know where your gauge is. So, start slow and low. We have 10 milligram capsules and things like that.

I definitely think you need at least 20 to 30mg to start with and then you build it from there.

Rowan @ Infinity CBD

It's a difficult one because it's hard in the industry as a retailer to give advice, whilst treading lightly around medical claims. But most of the time, you should be able to state how many milligrams per drop or a measurement on the dropper.

As a rough guide, most people we find will be on a dose somewhere between 10 to maybe 35 milligrams per dose. Most people coming in for a kind of mental health anxiety will be on the lower end of that. Most other people will be on the higher end for therapy for chronic conditions.

But it's a gauge, you know, I think starting there is a good idea.

Try to keep it consistent for a week and if you're finding that you're not quite getting what you want, just slowly increase that bit by bit for another week or two, until you see if you're getting to where you want. But if at that point you're not, you can go the other way and go a lot higher and work back.

But generally, people find what they need within those first couple of weeks.

Oren @ Kiara Naturals

Well, this is a tricky question because every human is different and individually the right amount of CBD for me might not be the right amount of CBD for you.

More than that, sometimes the right CBD for you isn't the right amount every day. But that will of course balance out. So, I always recommend to my patients, my customers, to start slowly with two to four drops twice a day at least for two to three days, seeing if they get that benefit.

If they do get the benefit, they should actually try reducing it by one or two drops a day. Maybe they overshot it and if they didn't, I recommend every three or four days to increase by two to four drops overall in the day until you find the right amount.

Jade @ Savage Cabbage

My advice to people is to start slow and steady, and if they feel that they want to increase the amount that they're having, then they should, and it's kind of like a stepped process, if you like.

I don't think that anybody should, who hasn't used CBD before, just go for the strongest strength and the most amount. I also think that is a false economy because you could benefit from using much less, which is going to save you money. So, I would encourage people to buy a Savage Cabbage 25 milligram per ml bottle.

I encourage everyone to start there, and you know, if you were to have one dropper a day, that's 25 milligrams a day. If you get to day four and you just can't put your finger on why you feel a bit different and you don't feel as good as you did yesterday, that to me is an indication that you need to top up or increase.

I ask people to keep a reflective diary so they know what they've had, how they felt, and so they can look back and go, actually my number is this and this is the amount that I feel that I require to go about my business. Obviously, it can peak and trough and change. But I think ultimately as a starting point, that that's where I would encourage people to go.

How quickly does CBD start working?

Sophie & Jess @ Canax Life

It can take anything from 15 minutes to 1-2 hours. Really, I think it depends what time of the day you have it. Have you eaten? How much have you eaten, etc.? So yes, anything from 15 minutes, you can feel a little bit of calmness coming over you.

Ben@ CBD Brothers

It can depend. It's very much different from one person to the next. The method of administration also plays a big part. If you're vaping and using CBD, that tends to have a slightly more instantaneous effect. If you're taking capsules, it has to work its way through your digestive system, so that can take a little while. I don't think there's a short, sharp soundbite answer for that.

I think it's dependent on the condition, the method of taking it, and what you are treating.

Matt @ Kloris CBD

It can be very much down to the individual and what you are taking it for. So, we see some people who will try CBD oil for the first time, and they will notice an effect within 10 to 15 minutes. We've had people come into the store, buy the product, walk out, try it, literally come back after having done a lap of the block and be like, I want to buy more, this is amazing.

With things like our topical products, they can be very fast acting because they're getting to work on the local area. For other people, if you are taking it for something that is a more deep rooted systemic issue and your endo-cannabinoid system is really out of balance, it can take a while.

So, we generally advise people to use products for at least a month to see the optimum effect. CBD does build up in your tissues over time as well. So, the effects should be compounding after a while.

It's also very much down to the individual and your sensitivity to it, and if you were taking it with supplements, medications, things like that.

You don't necessarily expect an instant result, particularly if you're taking things like vitamins for example, which is a good comparison in some ways. So, it's important to give it time, give your body a chance to adjust to it and be a little bit patient in waiting to see the full benefits.

Paul @ Herbotany Health

Obviously, I can only talk from my own personal experience but I can quite honestly say certainly ingestible products, like tinctures, are pretty quick.

If you're taking them for anxiety or sleeplessness or insomnia, I think you would feel the benefits within an hour or two of taking the product. It really does depend on the product though, but certainly on ingestibles, relatively quickly.

Paul @ Naturecan

It depends on the format that you take. So, if you vape, almost instantly you start to feel relief. Sublingually, if you like an oil, then it absorbs through the mucus membranes. It takes between 10 -20 minutes before you start feeling the effects.

Edibles take longer, going through your stomach.

There's less research into topicals, but usually when it's with something else, like we do an arnica cream and we do a chilli heat cream, you start to feel the relief from the chilli straight away and the CBD starts kicking in as well afterwards.

Rowan @ Infinity CBD

It depends on how you take it. If you were to hold CBD oil under your tongue, it's being absorbed straight into your bloodstream.

So general onset is typically within five to 10 minutes. But what's to be noted is that won't necessarily absorb the full dose. When you swallow the remainder of the CBD, or if you were to just take an edible, it can take anywhere between 40 minutes to two hours to kind of kick in.

The reason being is that it's going through your liver to be absorbed. So, it's just a longer process. But the upswing to that is, in theory, customers find that it's in their system for longer via that method. So, the method of taking CBD has a big impact on how fast the onset is, but also how long it lasts in your system.

Oren @ Kiara Naturals

Usually, ingestible CBD will take anywhere between 30-60 minutes to start working. It really depends on what you've been eating and what you're suffering from.

I find that for anxiety and stress, it works within those 30 -60 minutes. For more complicated problems such as sleep disorders or systemic inflammation, it will really take a few days until you can feel the benefits.

As far as vaping goes, that's a very easy way to get immediate relief for things like pain and stress because the absorption is so quick, it's in your bloodstream within a few seconds.

Jade @ Savage Cabbage

So, it's very much dependent upon the individual and unfortunately you only get to hear the stories about the people like me who've had a miraculous and very quick response to these products. That's really rare.

So, some people will say, give it a fortnight or give it four weeks.

If the products that you are using haven't given you any real benefits within three months, then it's recommended that you try a different one, because it might be a strain that doesn't suit you.

I think on average, we tend to notice from our community that it takes between two and three weeks to experience results.

So the immediate impact is quite rare. The only time that people really tend to notice an immediate impact is if they're battling with extreme anxiety that comes and goes, but when it arrives, it's like a punch to the chest.

If they take their CBD at that time, we've had it reported back to us that they feel like it melts away like butter.

That was the moment where they were like, this does actually work because I was having a bit of a crisis. I've had my oil and now it's gone away. And that's brilliant. So, I know that it works for that.

But I would always encourage people to give it at least a month.

How long should I keep taking CBD for?

Sophie & Jess @ Canax Life

I think that's dependent on the actual consumer. Research suggests that taking it daily and letting it build up in your system is the best way to take it. We do have customers that take it ad hoc, and it works for them for certain times of the month or pain relief.

But mostly the benefits of taking it daily and for a few months, building it up, is the most beneficial way to take CBD.

Ben@ CBD Brothers

For as long as it takes to help, is the short answer. If it stops working and you know it's not helping, then have a little bit of time off it and then per-haps go back to it.

But it's just down to the individual. If it stops working, stop taking it and then give yourself a 10 day break and then give it another go, see if it helps again. It's possible you've built up a bit of tolerance.

Matt @ Kloris CBD

As long as they are seeing a benefit from it at the end of the day. I think that is the key thing. It should be all about 'is this serving its desired function?' Is this helping you in the way that you want?

If it is, then continue taking it by all means. If you feel compelled to exper-iment with altering your dosage or your timings or how frequently you are taking it, if you're not seeing the benefit, you should evaluate that and maybe try something else.

It's going to be down to the individual and your individual response to it. You shouldn't feel that if you've started taking it, you have to keep taking it. I think it's very important to consider this holistically, in the context of everything else that is going on in your life, so this is just part of the puzzle.

So, if you've managed to solve the other stress factors that you had, and therefore you're feeling much more relaxed, then you probably don't need to be taking CBD for stress. But if everything else in your environment is the same, then you probably still need that bit of assistance from it.

Paul @ Herbotany Health

I believe it really does depend on what your particular reason is for taking CBD. I would suggest, for long-term ailments, possibly giving CBD a try for a prolonged period of time, particularly if you are feeling benefits from it.

But for other short term ailments, like anxiety or something like that, then as and when required, but personally I'm a big advocate of taking it regularly.

Paul @ Naturecan

Some people take it for difficult periods in their life, sort of mentally, emotionally. Some people take it for recovery after sort of operations and things like that.

But what we find is that most people, once they start taking it, it's for overall wellness. I try to describe the endocannabinoid system as your air traffic control system for your body. So, you wake up with a bad shoulder, bad neck, that's what sends the message to your receptor's, you know, 'relieve here'.

The best benefits of CBD are when you constantly take it and it's always in your system. It doesn't have to be huge amounts, but take it regularly.

I've been taking it for five and a half years now. I've never felt better. Even to the point I give it to my dad, my mom with all my family taking it.

My dad says that three years ago it used to hurt to pull his socks up in the morning, because he was getting old and everything else, and he just doesn't feel those aches and pains anymore and he sleeps better, he doesn't wake up in the night.

So, you know, obviously anecdotal, but we've also got thousands of reviews that say the same thing.

Rowan @ Infinity CBD

With our customers, who are coming in for all kinds of more chronic conditions, we always say give it a good couple of weeks, just to see if this is something that's going to be useful for you. Whereas others, who aren't using it as frequently, it's kind of an as and when they need it.

So, it can vary greatly depending on the specific needs. I'd say half of our customers are people that are using it as a replacement for other things, kind of semi permanently, and the other half are people who are using it maybe once or twice a week, maybe just on the weekends or around a particular instances or events that can be more straining or stressful for them.

Oren @ Kiara Naturals

I think that first of all, as it has no real undesired effects and as long as it's making you feel better, you should take it for as long as you feel comfortable.

Once your issue is resolved or drastically improved, I would see how it feels without it to see if you still need it. There is no set time frame. Every condition here is different. I would also not expect CBD to solve my problem. It's a great help. It's a great remedy.

Jade @ Savage Cabbage

As long as you feel you need to, whereby you could start using a product today and use it for three months, feel great and go, 'I don't actually need to use this anymore'.

So, stop, give yourself some time off. Then you'll probably find within six to eight weeks that you are wanting to go back to repurchase, to get back to where you were previously.

But it's very much dependent on the individual. I would never say to anybody, you've got to take this for the rest of your life, because who am I to say that, it's none of my business.

I would support anybody that wanted to go through a couple of months on, or a couple of months off. Whatever works for that person. It is a per-

sonal kind of journey. Everybody's experience is very, very different. That's kind of how I would approach that.

How can I understand the different strengths of CBD?

Sophie & Jess @ Canax Life

So, the milligrams of CBD in a product are just referring to the metric amount of cannabinoid in that product. This is much more straightforward when it comes to edibles rather than oils.

Our gummies, for example, have 25mg of oil coating per gummy.

And our Mellow Meno capsules have 20mg of CBD, and our Hey Hormones, will have 30mg of CBD per capsule.

Ben@ CBD Brothers

It's best to check the company website. And if you've got any issue or concerns, speak to the company. If they're a good company, which falls in with some of the other questions, they'll be able to assist you.

Oren @ Kiara Naturals

Well, this is actually both complicated and easier than it seems. You should start by comparing similar size products, for example 10ml, or 30ml.

But then it's very different when it comes to concentration. The concentration is the proportion of CBD we have inside. If I have a 10ml bottle, with 10% strength CBD, this will mean that there is 1000mg or one gram of CBD in that bottle.

Now, if you really want to calculate how much you have inside, what you should do is know the amount of drops that are in the bottle. A 10ml bottle will traditionally have between 200 and 230 drops.

While a 30ml bottle will have three times as much, about 670 to 680 drops.

So, you take the total amount of CBD you have, which you can understand from your percent. Let's say you have a 10% strength oil in 10ml, that will be 1000mg.

You divide that by the amount of drops, and then you'll know how much is in each drop, and then you can dose very accurately.

There are three factors you need to know. How much oil is in my bottle, 10ml or 30 ml. What's the amount of CBD inside, the milligrams or the grams and this I know from the percent and how many drops are in there. Then you can accurately calculate how much CBD you're getting with every drop.

Matt @ Kloris CBD

I think it's important that we separate ingestible products from topical products because the percentages mean wildly different things in those two scenarios.

So, let's focus on ingestible products, which is typically where you're going to be looking at a specific dose that you want to take.

The easiest way with something like oil drops is to break it down per drop of that product so you know how many milligrams of CBD you're getting. So, we keep it super simple.

We only do two strengths of CBD, for example, we do a 5% and we do a 10%.

In the 5%, you're getting 2.5mg per drop. In the 10%, you're getting 5mg per drop. You can work out your dosage very easily. And that's the only thing that matters.

Generally, a lot of brands will say how many milligrams of CBD are in the product that you are buying because I think it gives a perception of the value of that product. But it's important to remember that it is the total amount in that container.

So, 1,000mg in a 30 ml bottle is one third of the strength per drop of a 1,000mg and a 10ml bottle. If you break it down to what is the strength per drop it's the simplest way to work out your dosage.

Paul @ Herbotany Health

That's a great question and my advice would be to use a brand which has both milligrams and percentages quite clearly stated on their packaging.

Paul @ Naturecan

We've got a big range, so we've got everything from a 5% right up to a 40%.

The key goes back to milligrams. On our bottle, we've got how many milligrams there is per drop, but it is difficult to work out especially given the different sized formats as well.

So 1,000mg in a 10ml bottle is 10% strength, a thousand milligrams in a 30ml bottle is obviously 3% and that's where the confusion comes in.

It's always worth measuring exactly how many milligrams is in each bottle. What we tend to find as well is that people start off buying a 5% and a 10% and then eventually, because of the huge cost savings, end up at a 20% or 40%, and they take less of it.

So, if you're taking four drops of a 20% strength, you can take two of a 40% and it costs you half the price or a third of the price, something like that. So, we have a lot that migrate through the strengths.

Rowan @ Infinity CBD

Yes, it's definitely not an ideal and easy way to learn how to calculate it. What I would say is these days, any reputable brand should have done these calculations for you on the label, hopefully.

But really, all you are interested in is the milligrams. Therefore, you can kind of work out on the back either per drop or if there's a measurement on it from the dropper.

I'm sure most companies are happy to answer any questions specifically if you're still struggling to do the maths on it.

I'm hoping there's going to be a universal approach that makes this much easier for everyone to understand. Education is key to just back this up and kind of reinforce why it's important to make this simpler for the consumer to work.

Jade @ Savage Cabbage

This drives everybody around the twist. So, to keep it simple, a bottle of Savage Cabbage 1000mg in a 10ml bottle, where the 1000mg references that there's 100mg of CBD per one ml of liquid, that equates to 10%.

Our bonus questions...

After we'd asked our Experts the 20 Questions, we decided to throw in a few Bonus questions - just for fun and also to get their personal opinions and perspective...

What's your favourite way to take CBD and why?

Sophie & Jess @ Canax Life

I think we've both agreed on this, we've tried the oils before and they've never agreed with us.

Hence why we started with gummies and I think that's our favourite way of taking it, just because it's a nice treat to have rather than a bag of sweets.

Our gummies work effectively. We've never really been into vaping. I've never vaped CBD, so I think gummies are definitely our favourite.

Ben @ CBD Brothers

I like the Oil droppers. They're old school. You know where you are with them and you can pretty much work out what your dosage is.

I like the taste, I love the earthy, hashy, cannabisy taste. There's nothing about CBD oil under the tongue that I don't like, so I'm a big fan.

Matt @ Kloris CBD

It's got to be patches, because it's just such a convenient method. I use our 24 hour patches and it's just, one a day and its way of me being certain that I am getting a daily maintenance dose of CBD.

We also have things like turmeric and Resveratrol and Amiga in there as well. So that's really great for joint support as well.

I just find them an incredibly convenient method, especially for fitting into my lifestyle. I've got a young infant at home, so it's really useful to know I'm sorted.

Paul @ Herbotany Health

Herbotany Health 50mg capsules because I absolutely recommend them, and they have been life changing for me.

Paul @ Naturecan

Absolute favourite is oil. I take that every night. I'm terrible for liking confectionery, as soon as I open a pack of gummies I just keep going back for more and more.

Chocolate as well, but oil's my favourite. I'm going to probably list 20 different products now, but I go for the edibles. I love nut butters. I love the chocolate and the gummies, you know, they're my favourite fun format.

Rowan @ Infinity CBD

I'm a coffee lover, so being able to add CBD to my coffee in the mornings is quite a nice part of my day just because it symbolises my enjoyment of the coffee, as well as kind of kickstarting how I feel a bit.

You know, I use CBD oil as a baseline with drops. But if I'm getting to the end of a tough week and I'm feeling a bit beat up, I can admit I don't mind having a nice bath where I can soak in it a little bit.

So, I think that's probably my kind of secret enjoyment, I guess, is making a little CBD bath bomb. I can get in on a Saturday night and just relax.

Oren @ Kiara Naturals

Well, I find that there are two sides to that question. The most fun way to take it is gummies. I love our CBD gummies. I love gummies in general. I try not to eat too much sugar, but gummies are just, with CBD, I'm like, ah, it's healthy, it's sweet, it's great, I love that lime flavour.

That's fantastic. But for me, the most beneficial way to take CBD is actually in a hydro ethanol tincture, not in a carrier oil. I find that absorption is better - I find that it works faster.

Jade @ Savage Cabbage

I like the tinctures because I think familiarity of where I started - and that's how I started.

I like the fact that if I am feeling a bit anxious that I know it's going to work quickly. It's just my natural go-to.

But like I say, I do have gummies upon my person at all times. I do like to have two gummies throughout the day, but the tinctures are my go-to favourite.

What do you dislike about the CBD market, products or industry?

Sophie & Jess @ Canax Life

There's a few things! I think before we started the business, we didn't real- ise there's so much unknown about it and when people say, 'what do you do?' and we tell them and they say, 'oh, isn't that drugs and stuff?' you're like, no, we're not drug dealers!

CBD has a really bad connotation with the drugs industry and that is be- cause of THC. So, you know people read snippets here and there and they come to assumptions about it without really knowing the full facts.

There's also a lot of red tape around CBD, which prohibits you from selling on all sorts of platforms and marketing is really difficult. However, that is changing and that will be changing I think in the coming 12 to 24 months.

That's what we both find really frustrating, but I think that will all change in the coming years. We're spreading the word and delivering knowledge, information, and wonderful stories of success to hopefully change people's thinking.

Ben@ CBD Brothers

I may have mentioned I have a real thing about stuff being sold in garages.

It really frustrates me when I see shots of CBD or little CBD things in garag- es, because it's not going to do anything for you. It's more than likely crap CBD and it doesn't do our industry any good. It doesn't belong in a garage. It's not a cigarette product, it's not a shot of energy drink.

Slick marketing campaigns, they get on my nerves a little bit because I kind of wish I'd thought of that before them! But that's really as far as it goes. I know there's some things that make me a little bit annoyed because I didn't think of it first. Trip CBD are quite good at that because they've got this lovely, wonderful, dreamy packaging.

Also, the nonsense that's told. There's a lot of bullshit in the industry and there's a lot of people that try and put each other down, which is what I try to stay away from.

Matt @ Kloris CBD

My pet hate about the CBD industry is a lot of brands out there making outlandish claims.

I hate it when people are putting CBD into products where it makes no sense and using that as a marketing tactic. So, for example, people who are putting CBD into ridiculous things like pillow sprays, where that is not going to get into your system.

I've seen over in the States. There were people who were putting CBD into things like mattresses. How on earth is that supposed to get into your body? Because surely, you're putting a sheet on your mattress and you might be wearing bed clothes, so there is no way on earth that is going to give you any benefit.

Candles are another good one. You're literally just setting it on fire. You are never going to get that into your system.

Paul @ Herbotany Health

Companies who aren't as committed to a regulated industry as companies like my own Herbotany Health. And synthetic CBD.

Paul @ Naturecan

I think one of the things that I hate in the industry the guys that are in it for the cash and grab, you know, they've come into a market that they've thought, wow, this is going to be incredible.

They make terrible products and are just looking to make a quick buck basically. Whereas there's plenty of good players in the industry that are, over a 20/25 year timeframe, growing their brands and building this industry up. So that would be my sort of biggest pet hate I'd say.

Rowan @ Infinity CBD

I think, and this is no fault of anyone particularly within the industry, but there is a big divide. I'm painting with broad brush strokes here, but the divide is primarily between big money, big firms, and big marketing, and people who are coming in from a more naturalistic approach because they're a grassroots movement.

There's quite a lot of disparity between the two. There's paranoia from one side, that big pharma is coming in and encroaching on how things are and looking down on how certain things are going, whilst smaller companies are just trying to kind of get their grasp on the industry.

My pet peeve is seeing that kind of debate online in a really negative manner instead of one that's more collaborative. Because the last three years of the industry have been really rocky with the change of Novel Foods and no one's known what's going to happen next.

Being able to work hand in hand more collaboratively, to establish things like how you work out your dosage across all labels, so consumers are clear on it, are the kind of things that we really should be focusing on, rather than trying to shoot down other people, that ultimately are also just trying to establish the industry that we all want to thrive in.

So that's my only pet peeve I think I really have, because it's a shame to see this happening, but that isn't to say that we haven't had lots of really positive experiences collaborating with people on all scales of the industry, but it will just be nice to see more of it now that things are settling down here.

Oren @ Kiara Naturals

Yes, I have specific ones for each of those. But let's start with the products. My pet hate is products with CBD oils with 3% or 5% CBD. I feel that those are damaging to the industry.

I feel that the consumers are not getting the benefit that they should be getting, and I feel like in the end, even though they don't know if they're getting ripped off for the money, that's a real big hate of mine.

The second hate that I have is the lack of responsibility that brands are having towards the fact that we are helping people with medical conditions, even though officially we're not.

But we are there to support people with their pain, anxiety, with their loved ones. We are giving them tools that are changing their lives and we must own up to that responsibility, which most of the industry does not.

A third favourite hate on the industry is that the industry is behaving like a new industry in the nineties. There's no social agenda. There is no environmental agenda. It's a plant and this plant is an incredible plant that can be used to change the world, and we are twisting it into a commodity that is just generating more plastic and garbage.

Those are my three hates. Sorry if that's a bit intense, but that's what I feel. The cannabis industry should be a light for consumerism.

Jade @ Savage Cabbage

I think my pet hate in all honesty, is that there are many, many people like myself that set up a business to help people and those people have been squeezed out of the way by big money that set up sexy brands with massive marketing dollars, and they don't necessarily have the heart space because they see it as the green rush.

I think it's a crying shame that there are many small businesses that have not survived this Novel Food process and it's paved the way for bigger companies to come in and claim that space. And I think that's really sad.

What other CBD brands do you respect and why?

Sophie & Jess @ Canax Life

Ever since building our brand, we absolutely love Kloris CBD, I just love the look, it's so professional.

The website is educational, ethical and the products are amazing. Their skin products and everything are amazing. So we definitely think that's one of our most favoured.

Ben@ CBD Brothers

I used to have an issue with Simply CBD because they copied our colouring and stuff like that, but I got to speak to Brian, who was the owner (I'm not sure if he still is) and the man is amazing. He's a really good guy.

He does everything for the right reason. He's in it for helping dogs that he's rescuing. So, I've got a lot of time and respect for him and Simply CBD.

Dutch Natural Healing is really good. They've been doing a lot of good things in the industry for many, many years.

Generally speaking, if it came to who I respect, it would be British Cannabis. I find my only issue with British cannabis is they do a lot of their stuff in Portugal, so technically it's not British cannabis, in the same way that we are not in Britain because we farm in Guernsey. But again, they've been there for a long time and they're really pushing the boat out and they're really doing good stuff.

Companies like Little Hemp Shop as well, they do a lot of grass roots stuff and they really help organise and keep communities together with their Facebook pages.

I like the National Hemp Service, who are doing lots of good stuff promoting cannabis and things like that.

I like people that put it on the high street and make the effort to get in there, not just go into Holland and Barrett and stuff like that, but actually, they put their money where their mouth is, like we have.

This is a raw, productive, serious product and compound that needs to be taken very seriously and all of those companies I've mentioned have done the best to help put that out there in their own little way.

Matt @ Kloris CBD

I really like what the team at Trip are doing in terms of opening up the market. I think they've done it very well for their target market, which is definitely a younger market than ours.

I think they've gone about it in a really interesting way that's clearly resonating with the market. I view that as like they're giving people a bit of an entry point into the potential of CBD but taking it into more of a lifestyle thing.

Paul @ Herbotany Health

Any member of the ACI.

Paul @ Naturecan

So, there's definitely a couple here and you know, obviously, Naturecan is the best brand out there, chaps, we know that.

But you know, I love Trip the drink. I think it's fantastic what they're doing. I love the sort of marketing that they do as well and everything else.

Medterra in the States, I've got a lot of respect for them because they've been innovative with the products as well, they've got nice chocolate and edible products as well.

Rowan @ Infinity CBD

We've had quite a lot of different brands in our shops since we opened, Infinity CBD isn't the only product that we sell, so there's quite a few that we've used over the time and we've had a lot of really positive feedback so it's hard to ignore the fact that, you know, there are products some people will get on better with than our own.

You know, we're not here to just keep on plugging our own stuff. CBD Brothers have been a really prominent one.

I think they're coming from a similar background to us where it's grass-roots, it's coming from people who use it. So, they kind of are coming from a place where they really empathise with the end user rather than the sales.

Having used some of their balms that have a stronger terpene profile due to the way that they extract it, there's no arguing that it's certainly a really, really good product. And it's great to see that kind of stuff in the UK.

So, off the top of my head, probably them at the moment.

Oren @ Kiara Naturals

Well, I really respect Charlotte's Web. First of all, it's the biggest and you know, you have to give thanks to the elders that have paved the road for you and they basically were one of the first, so I respect that. I also like their branding.

Cannadoca is a brand that I really admire. They do so much more than just selling and manufacturing CBD. They have educational centres. They are repopulating indigenous European hemp into nature and they're really doing a fantastic job.

Jade @ Savage Cabbage

There is a brand out there. It's a UK brand and they're called Mindful Extracts. And I like them because I've got to know some of the people involved in that brand and they share similar moral stances to myself.

They want to help people, they want to build a community, and they've got a really nice Instagram page. They've put out really lovely self-care tips and clips and things like that. And I just, I just like them. They're just very honest, very modest, and they've got a moral compass. I think that they tick those boxes for me.

If you could make CBD taste of anything, what would you choose?

Sophie & Jess @ Canax Life

Well, chocolate obviously, and you can infuse chocolate with CBD. So Yeah, we both discussed what it would be, and chocolate was the number one for the both of us.

Ben@ CBD Brothers

Just more 'cannabisy'. I love the taste of cannabis, it's a beautiful thing. I don't want it to taste of anything apart from cannabis. If I'm taking CBD and it tastes like strawberry, I don't get that.

Let's have it taste like actual cannabis, shall we? Because then we know what we're doing, and we know where we're at. And it also sets a marker of quality in the product.

If it doesn't taste of cannabis, then I'd be lying about where the hell it's coming from, or what else they'd put in it to make it not taste like cannabis.

Matt @ Kloris CBD

I think that would be down to personal preference. In terms of its raw form, I don't mind the taste. I actually find it quite pleasant.

Maybe that's because I've been taking it for so long. I don't know that I would want to change it to be honest. I like it in its natural form.

Paul @ Herbotany Health

Although I take our capsules, which are tasteless, I think natural flavour is preferred for me.

Paul @ Naturecan

It's going to be something sweet. As you can imagine, it's our watermelon gummy. It just doesn't get any better than that.

We've got different fruit flavours and it's just about pips the rest of them, it's the watermelon for me.

Rowan @ Infinity CBD

That's interesting. I quite like the taste of CBD, the kind of nutty flavour to it. I really enjoy cooking so I find that I've been pairing it with things that I make at home, like salad drizzles and marinades that compliment certain tasting profiles.

I find it quite exciting how much variation there is in the smell and taste.

If I had to change it, it would just be for those customers that just don't get on with it and make it kind of more palatable.

So, whether that would be a plain flavour, I don't know, but certainly something to help those people that don't get on with it.

Oren @ Kiara Naturals

I rather it just tastes the way it does. I would keep it as the most bitter original CBD extract because those alkalines and those bitters, they're very medicinal.

I've been drinking different plants and plant extracts for so long that for me, that flavour is like, that's high quality.

Jade @ Savage Cabbage

Hmm. That's a difficult one for me to answer just because I have food issues because of my gastrointestinal disease, but my favourite flavour is the Madagascan vanilla.

Because it's so unique.

There's nothing else like it on the market and it's produced in such a way that it's so organic and so pure that it's almost like eating ice cream.

It's really nice. And I'm quite happy with that, but I just think that flavour profiles are something that I've spent too much time thinking about personally, just because of personal circumstances.

Which food would you like to see infused with CBD?

Sophie & Jess @ Canax Life

I think definitely any flavour chocolate with CBD in would be amazing.

Ben@ CBD Brothers

I think the more food infused with CBD, the better. I think if we could get some nice butters we could do all kinds of little bits and pieces.

I've had CBD infused ice cream or cannabis infused ice cream before, that's been really nice. Obviously chocolate, that's already done. I think just about anything that's got CBD in would be really good.

Matt @ Kloris CBD

I think from a purely personal perspective, given that I have a young infant at home and I largely live on black coffee, CBD infused coffee would be a huge win for me.

Paul @ Herbotany Health

Sausages!

Paul @ Naturecan

Interesting timing on this question because last week at a conference, I had a steak that was infused with CBD butter. They poured the CBD butter over the steak as it was served, it was incredible.

The steak was brilliant as well, but with the CBD, because it's like a slightly earthy taste, it was incredible. I did also have some great CBD drinks too and they were also infusing CBD into puddings. There were cannabinoids in different courses of the meal, so just incredible.

Rowan @ Infinity CBD

I think it's an interesting one and funnily enough, there was a recent study done on it, about introducing CBD in different ways into the food chain essentially.

There has always been a debate about whether we are so adapted to these cannabinoids, in terms of our system due to agriculture in our history. If you're talking about cows for example, using their biomass for hemp, then is there any kind of translation naturally through the food chain in that sense? Sure enough, they've just found that THC and CBD are transferable through to the milk.

It's a strange one, but I think perhaps looking at it, if there's any way to have benefits to having the unique spectrum of cannabinoids through different systems like that, the theory being that potentially that's how our ancestors used to most commonly interact with these cannabinoids, if that makes sense.

But beyond that, I'm pretty set with chocolate because it tastes great. I can't go wrong with that.

Oren @ Kiara Naturals

Ooh, I think pasta with pesto!

Jade @ Savage Cabbage

Okay, so I have got a complex gastrointestinal disease. So, I'm very limited to what foods I can actually have, but I start my morning with a granola and yoghurt combination. If I could get a yoghurt infused with CBD, I would be the biggest buyer of it.

SECTION FOUR

Our CBD Experts

Our CBD Experts have all been involved in the CBD market in the UK for a number of years and have created successful CBD brands, driven by their passion to create the highest quality products.

Their knowledge, experiences, and insights have really helped us understand both the opportunities and challenges associated with creating and growing a successful CBD brand and business.

Our featured experts are:

Sophie and Jess, co-founders of Canax Life

Ben Birrel, co-founder CBD Brothers

Matt McNeill, co-founder of Kloris CBD

Paul Batchelor co-founder Herbotany Health

Paul Finnegan, co-founder Naturecan

Rowan Bailey co-founder of Infinity CBD

Oren Landa, co-founder of Kiara Naturals

Jade Proudman founder of Savage Cabbage

Expert Brand Profiles

You can learn more about each of these brands in our CBD Brand Directory on the website:
www.cbdgenie.uk/cbd-directory

or by scanning the QR code.

SCAN ME

Sophie and Jess, Canax Life

Sophie and Jess have created a CBD business based on their own experience and that of close family members. When Jess's mum was diagnosed with multiple myeloma, a type of bone marrow cancer, she was desperate to find something to help with her mum's daily anxiety and sleeping patterns.

Joined by her friend Sophie, a nurse by trade, who had seen first-hand the life changing impact of CBD, their journey began.

These two ladies are dedicated to providing the highest quality CBD products under the motto "less of the stress". They see this as a journey, helping people with everyday struggles to change the often crazy chaotic world that we live in.

CBD Product Portfolio

While CBD is the main element of the company's products, this has been infused with an array of different ingredients to create enticing aromas. Gummies to bath bombs, capsules to gift packages and bundles, the range of products continues to grow.

CBD Gummies

There is a large range of Gummies including flavours such as strawberry, sour apple, zero, watermelon sugar and cherry pop. Each product page contains all the information you require such as ingredients, storage information, detailed product description and a reminder as to how CBD works. Gummies have become a very popular means of ingesting your daily CBD intake, something you can slip into a pocket and chew on at any time.

CBD capsules

Targeting the ladies market, Canax Life sell CBD capsules aimed at balancing hormones and assisting with the menopause. Vegan and vegetarian friendly, there is no unpleasant aftertaste with capsules available in 20 mg and 30 mg strength. The capsules can be swallowed or opened into a small glass of water, stirred and drunk. This product has proved to be extremely popular amongst those going through the change and impacted by hormonal imbalances.

CBD bath bombs

Initially CBD bath bombs were seen as something of a novelty item with many people unsure as tothe real benefits. However, the Canax Life CBD bath bombs come in three different flavours, lavender, orange, and rose, all of which are mixed with an array of different fragrances. They smell and feel like a typical bath bomb but within that is the mix of isolate CBD which is relaxing and soothing, helping with everyday stress.

Accessories, bundles and gift sets

Canax Life also offers a range of accessories, bundles and gift sets whether looking for a birthday gift or Christmas present. These are high quality products, which come with detailed ingredients and usage guidance. Unsurprisingly they are attracting very positive feedback from customers.

Canax Reviews

Whilst Canax are not on Trustpilot, they do have an extensive list of reviews on their website from verified customers. Within the 235 reviews listed on their website, 95% have given them five stars. And having sampled their products ourselves, it's not hard to see why.

We also had one of our CBD testers, Jenny, put the Canax gummies to the test and you can see that interview and review on our YouTube Channel (@cbdgenie) or via the QR code below.

Comment from Sophie

"Being from a medical background, for me, it's important to invest in the edu-cation side of the business. Obviously, we can't make claims, but we can give people easier access to the information and research that's already out there. So, we do a kind of science Sunday, where we pick a topic every week on our social media. We'll give research papers and answer questions so everyone can make an informed decision for themselves".

Canax Mummy Gummies

Watch the video on our YouTube channel **@cbdgenie** to see how one of our CBD testers got on with Mummy Gummies.

Or scan the QR code.

SCAN ME

Ben Birrell, CBD Brothers

Still managed by the original founders, CBD Brothers is the oldest provider of cannabis extracts in the UK.

The company started life in the founder's garage, mixing and blending cannabis extracts to help neighbours with an array of medical conditions.

With positive feedback and irrefutable evidence of success, the original CBD Brothers lotions and potions were flying off the shelves!

CBD Brothers was the first UK business licenced to grow full-spectrum cannabis and a leader in the introduction of THC-rich preparations into the food chain.

Through innovative and transparent forward thinking and backed by scientific studies, CBD Brothers is revolutionising the CBD landscape in the UK.

The company motto says everything, "Health over Wealth".

CBD Product Portfolio

It is fair to say that CBD Brothers provides what can only be described as a truly extensive range of CBD products. In addition, the company also offers a range of herbal remedies having partnered with leaders in this area.

CBD Oils

CBD Brothers offers a full range of CBD oils from 280mg up to 1200mg with each web page containing a detailed description of the product, down to the amount of CBD per drop. This is an impressive range with more than enough information to choose the right CBD strength product for you.

CBD Balms

The company offers an interesting range of CBD balms with varying strengths and a mix of CBD and herbal remedies. The original CBD Brothers balm is still available, incorporating organic coconut oil, beeswax, and CBD plant extracts. This is flying off the shelves!

CBD Capsules

All of the CBD capsules available on the website are vegan friendly with the CBD element ranging from 1400mg to 2500mg per bottle. Again, instructions and attention to detail is very impressive and helpful to consumers.

CBD Gummies

As well as offering CBD Gummies ranging from 10mg to 50mg of CBD per sweet, there is also a huge range of CBD infused chocolate. From mint to dark orange, Belgian white chocolate to a hot chocolate stirrer, the selection is impressive. Definitely worth a look!

Water-soluble CBD

The water-soluble CBD product has 40mg of CBD per ml of product and is very useful for those who prefer a drink alternative. CBD Brothers is one of a growing number of companies now providing water-soluble CBD.

Hemp treats for dogs!

Hemp-based treats for dogs is becoming a sizable market and CBD Brothers are tapping into this niche. The company sells hemp treats on the website that are vegan, hypoallergenic, gluten, and grain free - the perfect treat for your dog!

Trial sizes

CBD Brothers is one of the few companies to offer a range of CBD trial sizes for those concerned about buying in volume without trying the product first. An interesting and very useful concept!

Customer Reviews

There are approaching 500 reviews on the TrustPilot website with an average rating of 4.9, with 91% rating the company excellent.

The quality of CBD Brothers products is mentioned in detail, the immediate impact on physical pain and mental issues surprising many people. The company is proactive on the website, addressing questions and issues almost immediately.

Comment from Ben

During our interview with CBD Brothers, we asked co-founder Ben Birrell what makes CBD Brothers unique?

"I don't know if there are many other companies that are using British canna-bis. Growing, producing, extracting, and doing everything for themselves when we've always done that. I mean, we have labs where we do testing, and we are going through ISO accreditation at the moment.

As a genuine seed to bottle company it's interesting to look back at when we started in my garage. We haven't gone and taken someone else's product and then rebadged it or repackaged it as our own.

We've our core extracts and oils, all done by us. As far as I know no one else does this. What you see is what you get with us."

CBD Brothers Products

Check out the CBD Brothers portfolio on our website:
https://cbdgenie.uk/cbd-directory

Or simply scan the QR code.

Matt McNeill, Kloris CBD

The name Kloris comes from Greek mythology, the goddess of flowers from the islands of the Blessed.

Associated with spring, flowers, and new growth, this name fits perfectly into the company's mission to harness the healing power of CBD within an ethical and environmentally friendly scenario. Kloris uses only natural hemp extracts and avoids all of the fillers and preservatives seen with some CBD products.

Bringing together the founders, who all used CBD for various ailments, they created a personal mission and the basis for a very strong and growing company. The attention to detail, travelling round the world to see suppliers in action, and a very forward thinking approach to the environment has gone down well with customers. This is only the start of the journey for the Kloris founders, who believe that the benefits of CBD are still very much under-explored.

CBD Product Portfolio

There has certainly been a shift in the way in which CBD products are promoted, with many websites, including Kloris, allowing you to shop not only by product but by goals. For example, there are numerous products on the website if you are looking for help with sleeping or pain management. The range of products available includes:

CBD Oils

This is still the most popular area of the CBD market at the moment, with Kloris providing some classy products. Also available on subscription, you can buy high quality CBD oils in two different strengths, 5% and 10%.

CBD Skincare

Skincare products are now challenging CBD oils as the most popular in the market today. As well as supplying some traditional, non-CBD products, Kloris offers CBD balm, face oil/cream, eye cream, uplifting lotion, and various bundle packages. Certainly, worth a look!

CBD Patches

While oils, balm, and capsules are perhaps the most popular means of taking your daily dose of CBD, you can now buy 24-hour release patches and sleep support patches. The reviews for these particular products are impressive and this is an interesting diversion from the traditional market.

CBD Gift Sets

Now that the mystery and rumours surrounding CBD use have been corrected, it is now seen as an acceptable gift. Consequently, you won't be surprised to learn that Kloris offers a range of gift sets, providing a little of everything.

Customer Reviews

As with many CBD companies, we look forward to more feedback in the future with just 133 Trustpilot reviews available.

However, the overall Trust Pilot rating is an impressive 4.7 out of 5, with 90% giving the company a five-star rating and 4% posting a four-star rating.

Many of the comments highlight the quality of the products, the range, and the health benefits, but more importantly, a number of those leaving feedback have been recommended by friends. The Holy Grail of marketing!

Comment from Matt

"Our goal with Kloris is to create a premium brand. Something that people would be happy to show off and have on their shelf. Something they want to talk about and feel proud of using.

We've purposely positioned the brand really far away from the sort of cannabis style branding because that's not our aim.

It's a natural wellness brand we started from CBD, but we do work with a lot of other natural compounds now. We'd like to describe ourselves as, you know, the Aesop or the Rito of the wellness world. High quality branding with products created in a really sustainable and ethical way."

Kloris CBD Products

Check out the Kloris CBD portfolio on our website:
https://cbdgenie.uk/cbd-directory

Or simply scan the QR code.

SCAN ME

Paul Batchelor, Herbotany Health

Herbotany Health is the brainchild of friends and founders Paul and Danny, who both had very different experiences, but came together to build an innovative CBD company.

Using the company's partnerships in the US, they are delivering high-quality premium CBD products sold at affordable prices with a focus on sustainability. This ticks all of the boxes so far!

Paul's 30 years' experience in recycling and a deep-seated knowledge of the environment and sustainable products is behind their drive to create an eco-friendly, high-quality CBD company, which has become one of the leaders in the UK sector.

CBD Product Portfolio

Herbotany Health has taken a slightly different approach from its competitors, offering a core range of five products with different variations. These take in CBD massage oil, roll-ons, drops, salves, and capsules.

Luxurious CBD Massage Oil

This dermatologically tested luxurious CBD massage oil is handcrafted and incorporates high-quality CBD. It has been mixed with other oils that benefit the skin to create smooth, soothing, relaxing massage oil. Available in 50 ml and 100 ml bottles, the CBD element is a relatively low 1%, but you will still feel the benefit!

Opulent CBD Roll-On

Undoubtedly, innovation is the key to the success of the UK CBD market, with the Herbotany Health CBD roll-on proving extremely popular. Mixed with a variety of additional oils, some of which are proprietary, these are perfect for a quick boost to balance your body for the day ahead.

If you haven't tried a CBD roll-on yet, you will be surprised.

Premium CBD Drops

This is the core Herbotany Health CBD product, referred to as drops but otherwise described as CBD oils. Containing high quality, natural and sustainably sourced CBD, this product is proving to be extremely popular.

A wide selection of CBD strengths is available, taking in 3%, 5%, 10%, and 15%. While new products arrive regularly, CBD drops/oils remain the first choice for new converts and experienced CBD users.

Sumptuous CBD Salve

While salve describes products applied to the skin, it is more commonly referred to as balm or cream. This salve enhances the known benefits of CBD skincare products using high-quality CBD mixed with a coconut oil base and other essential oils. Yet another quality product added to the Herbotany Health CBD portfolio!

Superior CBD capsules

Amidst the range of new innovative products emerging in the CBD market, demand for traditional CBD capsules continues to rise.

They are still extremely popular and offer the ability to boost your CBD intake any time of the day, whether on their own, with a drink or with food.

The Herbotany Health CBD capsules are available in two different strengths, 20 mg and 50 mg per capsule.

Customer Reviews

Herbotany Health has an impressive average rating of 4.6 out of 5 on the company's Trust Pilot page. Interestingly, while there are just 35 reviews so far, the lowest feedback being 'Great' (11%) and with 89% of reviews rating the company as Excellent.

There are numerous comments on the full range of Herbotany Health CBD products, and the company is interactive on the review page.

Comment from Paul

"I think those responsible within our industry want it to be a world leader in terms of regulation and learn from the mistakes of other countries, whether it be recreational cannabis or CBD products from hemp.

We could go to the consumer and say, look, try this product. It's totally safe. It works. But the fact there's still not 100% clarity in the market for consumers is frustrating. However, I agree, it has been, in relative terms, a short amount of time to get where we are today.

The important thing is that the responsible companies survive and are able to reap the rewards of their investment in creating quality products - and proving to consumers that they are both safe and effective."

Herbotany Products

Check out the Herbotany Health CBD portfolio on our website:
https://cbdgenie.uk/cbd-directory

Or simply scan the QR code.

SCAN ME

Paul Finnegan, Naturecan

Those investigating the range of CBD products available will likely have come across Naturecan, a company which has websites in more than 30 different countries.

The group focus is based on three specific areas, product quality, customer safety, and supply chain transparency. However, when you begin to dig a little deeper you will notice there is much more to Naturecan!

The company was originally founded by Andy Duckworth and Paul Finnegan, who each bring specific skills and experience to Naturecan. Andy has an extremely impressive track record in the wellness business space, creating numerous online global leaders over the years. Paul is in charge of sourcing the best quality hemp, abiding by the ever-changing regulations, and creating and maintaining the crucial supply chain.

While there are now many more members of the Naturecan team, Andy and Paul are the leading lights, the innovators and they have a mighty impressive track record between them.

CBD Product Portfolio

It is safe to say that Naturecan has gone for a widespread approach to CBD products. When you enter the online store you will see CBD oils, snacks, balms, skincare, capsules, and bundled kits. There is a lot to choose from!

CBD Oils

There is a large selection of CBD oils on the Naturecan website varying in strength from 5% to 40% with a total of six different variations. All products are quality tested and it is safe to say whatever you need with regards to CBD oil, Naturecan can deliver. Even though we have seen a range of different products introduced to the CBD market, for many people, oils remain the focal point of the sector.

CBD snacks

The term CBD snacks will make many people chuckle, but you will be impressed at the range of products from Naturecan. These include CBD gummies, cookies, chocolate, brownies, and peanut butter.

There is growing demand for these types of products which offer a more convenient and tasty way to ingest CBD.

CBD balms

While often marketed under the term 'topicals', CDB balms are effectively a sub-sector in their own right. There is a huge range of CBD balms on the Naturecan website, including creams for muscles, joints, hand cream, lip balm, and even massage oils. There is strong research which shows how ingesting CBD via the skin can help concentrate the impact on muscles and joints.

CBD skincare

Where do we start with the range of CBD skincare on the Naturecan website! You'll find everything from CBD coconut shampoo to rose water, face cream to night-time cream, bath bombs to face sheets, and more. Whether looking to treat yourself or a friend, there is a lot going on in the CBD skincare world!

CBD capsules

The majority of CBD products on the Naturecan website are vegan friendly, which is reflected in the range of CBD capsules available. These include traditional capsules and softgels, with some infused with additional ingredients such as vitamins C. While capsules are seen as old school by many people they are still one of the more popular means of maintaining your daily CBD levels.

Customer Reviews

It is very rare for companies to offer quality affordable products while also maintaining one eye on the environment and the recycling of materials. However, with an average Trust Pilot score of 4.6, it is safe to say that Naturecan is one of those companies. A staggering 84% of customer reviews show a five-star rating with a combined 94% showing three stars and above. Where there are questions or queries, the company is very proactive on the website which also assists with customer satisfaction.

Comment from Paul

"In the UK, we have so many brands on the market, but they're all doing similar things, there is no real innovation. We have new products, and we want to launch more, but the regulations can sometimes hold us back. We want all of our brands to do well and help create this market because CBD does so much good for people.

If somebody takes CBD oil for the first time and doesn't like, or doesn't like the taste, that's it. So, we need to explore other ways and formats that people can access CBD. That's why capsules work well, as do edibles, gummies, and cookies. We do a brownie that you heat up slightly, and with a bit of ice cream you can eat them on the run. They're delicious!"

Naturecan Products

Check out the Naturecan CBD portfolio on our website:
https://cbdgenie.uk/cbd-directory

Or simply scan the QR code.

SCAN ME

Rowan Bailey, Infinity CBD

When you learn more about Infinity CBD, everything becomes clear. This is a company which has grown and developed with its long-term loyal customer base.

The trials and tribulations are well documented, together with competition in the industry and the need for constant innovation. This innovation has created a huge CBD product range which continues to grow.

Infinity CBD makes all cosmetic formulations from scratch, hand poured, and produced in small batches to retain control of quality. The attention to detail is mind blowing; the journey with customers is intriguing with the company open and honest about all areas of CBD. It is safe to say that the Infinity CBD journey still has some way to go, we can't wait!

CBD Product Portfolio

Like many larger companies in the CBD industry, Infinity CBD sells an enhanced range of CBD products such as oils, skincare, massage therapy, chocolate, tablets, and starter bundles. While initially CBD products were focused on CBD oil, this has spread to different areas of the market.

CBD Oils

The CBD oils section includes a range of different strengths from 2.5% to 40% across a range of different bottle sizes. From relatively mild to extra-strong, the range of CBD oils is impressive with some also focused on the vegan market.

CBD Skincare

CBD skincare is now a huge element of the CBD market and it is fair to say that Infinity CBD has jumped aboard this new trend. This section includes a range of different strengths from 250mg all the way up to 1000mg. Natural balms, massage oils and muscle relaxants, there's a good selection of CBD skincare products.

CBD Chocolate

In theory, you can infuse CBD into any solution so why not chocolate bars? This section includes a range of different flavours from orange and honeycomb to mint, dark raspberry to gingerbread and there are also some vegan CBD gummies. It is not difficult to see how people get addicted to these sweets!

CBD Tablets

While we have chocolate, oils, and CBD skincare products, many people are looking for a simple tasteless, easy to swallow CBD tablet. Infinity CBD provides full-spectrum CBD tablets with 25mg of CBD per capsule, perfect for dropping with your first coffee or tea of the day.

CBD Massage Products

Interestingly, the Infinity CBD massage products section is one of the largest in the online shopping area. From calming sticks to muscle relief, massage oil to a rest and relaxation bundle, there is a lot to choose from.

Customer Reviews

While relatively new to TrustPilot, there is a strong line of customer satisfaction running through the majority of feedback. Interestingly, pain relief and anxiety relief are discussed in equal measures in very positive terms. Many are surprised by the almost immediate impact, while others inquisitive as to why there is so much misinformation about the CBD industry.

Comment from Rowan

"What we're more focused on in the immediate future is the support groups and the products they have been able to use more frequently. We are looking to make it much cheaper for them to access these products.

That has been a big part of our ethos from the beginning. Like I said, we had £200 bottles whereas the equivalent we sell now is £49.99. We're trying to make our products as accessible as possible, looking at things that really help and last a while.

Actually, just going back to the education issues, we are looking at our core products, selling in a way that's more accessible and helpful to new people.

I think the biggest change we've seen is that when you supply the information to back up the product, customers really stick with it. They understand how to use it and that consistency really makes a difference between someone trying it and failing and trying and going, ah, I see how to use this.

You know, CBD for me isn't the same as popping a strong painkiller and within an hour like, oh wow, that's kicked in. It's more of something that you're trying to use to mitigate other issues and find more of a balance."

Infinity CBD Products

Check out the Infinity CBD portfolio on our website:
https://cbdgenie.uk/cbd-directory

Or simply scan the QR code.

Oren Landa, Kiara Naturals

Kiara Naturals co-founders Boaz "Bobo" Lehman and Oren Landa have built a fascinating company selling CBD products.

Based in the Swiss Alps the company grows, extracts, and formulates almost all of the certified organic hemp they use.

The mission is simple, to provide potent, high-quality products that maximise the evidence-based therapeutic natural remedies provided by CBD.

The products are GMO-free, free of pesticides, heavy metals, and artificial fertilisers and all certified via third-party testing. The dream began in 2005 when Boaz "Bobo" Lehman witnessed the immense power of CBD and other plant-based products.

Described as passionate alternative therapists, there is no doubt that the two founders have created a modern-day company based on a back-to-basics approach to medicine.

Product Range

The Kiara Naturals online shop offers an interesting option; you can buy by product type or shop by goal. For example, you can look at products which will help with pain relief, anxiety, sleep, skin, recovery or everyday health. Very helpful!

CBD Oils

The CBD oils come in a range of strengths, 5%, 10%, 20%, and 30% with very clear and concise instructions and a list of ingredients. There is also a useful list of ailments which these CBD products can help with such as stress, sleep, chronic pain, etc.

CBD Tincture

Tinctures are liquid herbal extracts which are used to tackle a number of health-based issues. Each 100ml bottle contains 1000mg of CBD together with additional extracts from five plants commonly related to assisting pain relief, sleep issues, and promoting relaxation.

CBD Topicals

While much of the focus tends to be on CBD oils, CBD topicals/creams are certainly a growing market with particular emphasis on muscles and joints and skincare/rehydration. The product pages are packed with key ingredients, which particular ailments they will assist with and the optimal dosages.

CBD Capsules

While many people prefer CBD oils there is growing demand for simple CBD capsules. Whether looking for a brain or body boost, or perhaps to enhance your immunity system, there are some interesting options.

Many people take these capsules with their morning brew to give them a good start to the day.

CBD Vapes

When you put together the innovative world of vaping and the up-and-coming world of CBD products, CBD vapes were the inevitable outcome. This is an extremely strong and growing part of the CBD market, one which is attracting significant interest.

Immunity Kit

While not CBD based, the Kiara Naturals website offers a very interesting immunity kit as a means of boosting your immunity system.

This contains an array of proven ingredients known to assist with fighting respiratory infections and boosting your immune system in general.

Customer Reviews

Even though there is no Trustpilot account as yet, there are literally hundreds of customer reviews on the website.

Even though some people are sceptical of on-site customer feedback, average ratings range from 4.5 out of 5 to a 5-star rating. It is obvious the company is focused on not only the products but also presentation, packaging, and overall customer services. This shows through as clear as day with honest customer reviews.

Comment from Oren

"We believe we are coming from a holistic point of view, where combining other compounds together can be beneficial, but only if there's the data and research to support it.

Why take just one ingredient when you can take a plethora of them and get the benefit from all of them. We see this in the hemp and cannabis world with pure versus full spectrum, right?

The full spectrum is a much more ancient, if we can call it that, and holistic approach. Pure hemp is leaning toward the pharmaceutical approach, single ingredients. So that for sure sets us apart.

We also have knowledge and experience of working with other plants.

I think the other part is the fact that we treat our customers in a different way. We try to give them the support to find out what they need and what they need it for. In many cases, CBD is the right thing, but if it's not, then there are many other things that can help.

Just try until you find the right dose, that's more or less our approach."

Kiara Products

Check out the Kiara Naturals portfolio on our website:
https://cbdgenie.uk/cbd-directory

Or simply scan the QR code.

SCAN ME

Jade Proudman, Savage Cabbage

Savage Cabbage offers a fascinating backstory having been founded as a community source for quality CBD, then expanding into a company with regular customers in 40 different countries.

Interestingly, the founders of Savage Cabbage have managed to maintain the family/community spirit within the business and drive forward using the company's core values.

The vision is to harmonise the connection between humans and natural healthcare.

The mission, to become a trusted provider of hemp, natural health, and wellness with a promise that they are more than just a retailer, they care about their customers.

Central to these core values is the belief that Mother Nature has the potential to improve quality of life, not just lifestyle.

This is a fascinating story of a small community operation which morphed into a company which has gone international.

CBD Product Portfolio

When you visit the Savage Cabbage website, you will notice the majority of products are from a company called Charlotte's Web. Originally formed in the US, this company offers complimentary CBD products to the Savage Cabbage CBD oil range with the combination proving very popular. Indeed, it was Charlotte's Web CBD products which prompted the founder of Savage Cabbage to start the business.

The combined range of products includes:

CBD Oils

The selection of combined CBD oils, taking in Savage Cabbage and Charlotte's Web, offers a range of CBD strengths and flavours from original to mint chocolate, orange blossom, and lemon twist. These are all exceptionally high quality CBD products with a raft of information about ingredients and dosage on each product page.

CBD Capsules

The Savage Cabbage website offers a range of CBD capsules which are proving to be extremely popular. While many choose flavoured oils and other CBD products, there is growing demand for plain CBD capsules. Many people choose to take CBD capsules with their early morning brew, a great way to start the day!

CBD Gummies

While the CBD gummies section is made up of Charlotte's Web products, this is a very interesting selection! The CBD strength ranges from 10mg to 15mg per sweet with a number of flavours including lemon lime, raspberry lime, lemon berry, and ginger. Many people have turned onto the idea of perfectly safe CBD infused sweets. Especially popular with those who have a sweet tooth!

CDB Topicals

When it comes to skin care, there are numerous medical reports which suggest that CBD is beneficial in many different ways. Consequently, the Savage Cabbage site offers a range of CBD topicals which include infused balm, roll-on, cooling gel, and cream. For those looking for more information, there is an in-depth analysis of the benefits of CBD on the Savage Cabbage website.

Customer Reviews

While the range of products on the Savage Cabbage site is predominantly from the Charlotte's Web brand, the overall Trust Pilot feedback is amazing. There are 818 reviews with an average score of 4.8 out of 5, very impressive.

There is specific mention about the quality of the products on sale as well as many references to the high standard of customer service. The number of satisfied customers continues to grow with 94% posting a five star rating.

Comment from Jade

"I think you mention the word cannabis and people panic because of its illicit use. It has been demonised for so long, that it's unfortunately got these negative connotations to it.

It's now about breaking through that barrier, legitimising the industry, and normalising self-care.I think it's a tide that needs to turn.

The reality is that cannabinoids are in all sorts of different foods as well as the cannabis plant.

So, now we're seeing the emergence of more medical cannabis clinics. That then causes confusion with what's medical and what's over the counter.

My approach to all of it is, yes, it's the same plant we're talking about, cannabis sativa, but the differentiating factor is the levels of THC in the product.

In the products that I sell, yes, there's THC, but it's under 0.2% and it's classified as hemp. There's a whole education process that needs to happen.

The thing is, the endocannabinoid system was discovered in the nineties, yet it's still not taught in medical school. Isn't that curious?

So, there are many levers that need to be pulled to action this change. I'm more than happy to sit and talk about that because it's a change that needs to happen."

Savage Cabbage Products

Check out the Savage Cabbage portfolio on our website:
https://cbdgenie.uk/cbd-directory

Or simply scan the QR code.

SCAN ME

SECTION FIVE

Top Ten Tips For Buying CBD

The first thing to understand when it comes to CBD is that all products are not created equally.

Amongst the CBD products available on the UK market, there are some that are definitely overpriced for what they are, and some that may be of inferior quality and may not deliver the desired outcome you're looking for.

So, in this section we want to share with you ten different ways you can assess and evaluate your choice of CBD product.

This will hopefully ensure you're getting the best value for money.

But this is not just about price, it's also about giving you the best possible outcomes by only choosing the highest quality products, from trustworthy brands.

After all, if you're looking to ingest your CBD either through oils, gummies or capsules, it's important to know what you're putting into your own body.

1. How do I avoid paying too much for my CBD?

If you're new to CBD, then it may first appear that all CBD products are excessively expensive. However, as you've probably already read in previous chapters, the production of CBD is both labour and process intensive, particularly when it comes to testing.

Additionally, CBD is still produced on a relatively small scale, so it's not mass produced.

Both these factors impact the price. But with that said, prices for CBD are coming down compared to previous years.

However there comes a point where the desire to reduce costs can impact on quality. So, it's definitely a balancing act.

If you're paying way below market price for your CBD, then this should raise serious questions about product quality. Inevitably some short cuts will have been taken in either the growing, production, or testing stages.

However, the same could be true with excessively high prices, as often this is more likely to be a case of marketing hype rather than increased product quality.

So, what should you be paying?

The best way to evaluate this is to take a look across a number of different brands and identify what is the average price - to establish a benchmark.

We would recommend using any number of the eight CBD brands we've collaborated with to put this guide together. All of these brands produce the highest quality CBD products and have the testing and processes to reinforce this.

If you look at the price of a 10ml bottle of CBD oil of the same strength (maybe 1000mg), from three or four different brands you'll get a feel for the market price.

So, whether you're looking to purchase your first CBD products, or looking to switch to an alternative brand for a change, you'll know what you should be paying.

2. What form of CBD should I use?

As you'll have read so far, CBD comes in many forms from the more standard formulations including oils, gummies, and capsules, through to the topicals such as creams, balms, and patches.

There's also the 'lifestyle' type of formulations which include things like chocolate, tea, coffee, and even CBD wine and beer.

And there's no doubt more to come.

Although with the current situation with regards to the FSA approvals, there are likely to be no new edible or consumable formulations coming to market within the next year or so.

However, the list of options for taking CBD is fairly extensive.

This makes it difficult for anyone to decide what form of CBD they should take in order to address their specific needs. And what will deliver the most impact in terms of improved health and wellness?

Having spoken to most of the CBD brand owners in the UK, this is a very common question. However, it's not one with a straightforward answer or one that can easily be addressed for the simple reason that it's down to our individual body chemistry.

The thing we have to remember is that CBD is a natural compound that interacts with your unique natural body systems. So, there is no single answer and no 'one size fits all' solution.

We can understand that on the face of it, this is not great news.

But we would suggest that there are some basic guidelines which you can use to help navigate through the plethora of options.

These are based on our own experiences and anecdotal stories from both brand owners and CBD users we've spoken with during the last year.

If we start with the basic premise that finding the right dosage and formulation of CBD for you as an individual, is a process of testing.

And then we group the formulations of CBD as follows:

Base level CBD

Localised CBD

Top-up CBD

Base level CBD

The base level CBD is your starting point, which is all about providing your body with a regulated amount of CBD, which you can then monitor and increase or decrease as required.

The formulation of CBD in this case are the ingestibles CBD oil, gummies, and capsules.

Most experts would suggest this is your starting point. We'll look at quantities and strengths in the next section.

Localised CBD

This is more specifically for localised short-term pain relief. In this case, you'll be looking at the topicals; CBD Oils, balms and now CBD patches.

These can be very effective in addition to your base level CBD by providing you with very localised short-term pain relief.

Having said that, the CBD patches now on the market are more designed for slow-releasing CBD over a longer period of up to 24 hours.

So, if you're at all concerned about ingesting CBD, the range of topicals could be your best option.

Topping up your CBD

In addition to the base level and localised CBD, there's a wide range of CBD products we'd categorise as Top-up CBD. These include a broad spectrum of innovative, interesting or possibly novel ways to take your CBD.

Whilst we personally wouldn't necessarily consider these as 'serious' CBD products, they do play an important role in helping more people discover and explore the wider benefits of CBD.

They also have the benefit of giving you a way to increase your CBD intake in a way that is both enjoyable and that fits with your lifestyle.

This is particularly highlighted with the introduction of both CBD wine and CBD beer!

3. How much CBD should I take?

The simple, but somewhat banal answer to this question, would be to take as much as you need.

But, we realise that's not very helpful. However, before we can start to explore this question, we need to cover some basics.

Firstly, in this guide, we cannot provide you with any personalised medical advice or recommendations.

The amount of CBD you may need to take will vary based on a number of individual factors such as body weight, medical history, other medications, and the intended use of your CBD.

And to make sure we cover ourselves, we would suggest it's best to consult with a healthcare professional before starting to take CBD, as they can provide personalised advice on dosing and any potential interactions with other medications you may be taking.

Additionally, it is important to follow the manufacturer's instructions on the product label.

With all that said, there are some basic guidelines we would suggest.

The UK Government's guidelines state that you should not exceed 70mg of CBD per day. But that doesn't automatically mean you should take, or in fact that your body needs 70mg of CBD to get the benefits you're looking for.

In all likelihood, you may not need anywhere near this level.

The other consideration is that your body needs time to respond to CBD, so finding the right amount for you will take a little time to figure out.

This is why we've suggested starting with some base-level CBD in the form of oils, capsules or gummies - as these are easy to take and regulate.

But the other rather large fly in the ointment here, is the fact that the amount of CBD you ingest (such as a 20mg gummy) is not the amount of CBD actually going into your body.

Because your body will only absorb a certain amount of the CBD you ingest. This is referred to as bioavailability.

The other thing to note is that some forms of CBD have a higher level of bioavailability than others. Typically, CBD oils have a higher bioavailability than gummies, which in turn have a higher bioavailability than topicals such as balms.

Here's it in a nutshell. Finding the right level of CBD dose for you, is down to experimentation.

However, all the Experts agree that it's best to start your dosage low, say at 10mg per day and stick with that for 3-4 days. If you're not feeling any benefit, then slowly increase your dose by 10mg every 3-4 days until you start to experience the results you're looking for.

Once you hit that level, it's just maintaining it.

But you can also top it up during the day if you feel the need to, using any of the available options previously discussed.

Taking this approach ensures you get the benefits, without wasting money taking unnecessary amounts of CBD.

4. When should I take my CBD?

Once again there is no universal answer to this question. Finding the best time of day to take CBD will vary depending on your personal preferences and the reason for taking CBD.

Some people find that taking CBD in the morning helps them start their day feeling more focused, while others prefer taking it in the evening to help them unwind and get better sleep.

However, you can take your CBD at either end of the day, or throughout the day. There are no set rules.

If you are using CBD for a specific condition or symptom such as for pain relief, then it is best to take the CDB when it's most needed. This is where the CBD balms and topical can be very beneficial as they can provide localised pain relief.

Once again, some experimentation is required to find the best solution for you.

As you can probably now appreciate, getting the optimum results or benefits from taking CBD is very much a personal journey, where you're experimenting with CBD formulations, strengths, and times of day to find the right solution for you.

When trying to find the best solution it's always advisable to try something for at least a few days, to see how it works, before deciding to move on to something else.

5. What type of CBD should I take?

We've so far looked at formulations of CBD, strengths and dosage, as well as bioavailability.

However, there's yet another component we need to throw into the mix. The type of CBD.

You've a choice between Full Spectrum, Broad Spectrum or Isolate CBD. Each type of CBD has its own advantages and disadvantages.Before we get into that here's a brief recap of each of these:

Full spectrum CBD.

Full spectrum CBD contains all of the naturally occurring compounds found in the cannabis plant, including CBD, other cannabinoids such as THC, terpenes, and flavonoids. The amount of THC is usually below the legal limit of 0.2%, which means it won't produce the psychoactive effects associated with marijuana.

Broad spectrum CBD.

Broad spectrum CBD is similar to full spectrum, but it goes through an additional refinement process to remove any trace amounts of THC.

This type of CBD still contains other beneficial compounds found in the plant, such as other cannabinoids, terpenes, and flavonoids.

CBD Isolate

CBD isolate is the purest form of CBD, as it contains only cannabidiol and no other compounds from the cannabis plant. It is typically extracted from hemp and then purified to remove any other cannabinoids, terpenes or flavonoids.

It seems there is little evidence that clearly points to one type of CBD being better than another.

However, many experts and enthusiasts firmly believe that staying as close as possible to the natural CBD extract is the most beneficial.

And the very small amounts of THC found in Full Spectrum CBD play an important role in delivering what is referred to as the Entourage Effect, where the combination of all of the components together can deliver something more valuable than they can individually.

With that said, Broad Spectrum CBD comes close to this with all the components of the full plant extract with the omission of the THC.

One thing to consider is that with any processing you are not just refining the product or compound, but the processing itself may modify the compound and potentially impact its effectiveness.

However, as with all things CBD, it's a personal choice and something for you to explore and experiment with.

6. What's a good CBD to try?

There are currently in excess of 50 different CBD brands available in the UK market, each selling dozens of different formulations in a range of strengths of CBD.

Which means you've literally thousands of products to choose from.

So how do you know where to start, or which brands to trust and try?

As I mentioned at the beginning of this section, not all CBD brands are equal, so it's important to do your research to ensure you're not overpaying, but you are getting a high-quality product that will deliver the benefits and experience you're looking for.

As CBD Genie we've talked to dozens of different brand owners, interviewed CBD experts and enthusiasts, and tried hundreds of different products, so we feel we have an understanding of what's out there and what to look out for.

In the next couple of chapters, we want to share with you some simple strategies to help you navigate the array of CBD products out there so you can objectively evaluate any brands you may be looking to buy from.

However, if you'd like a few recommendations to start with, then look no further than the eight CBD Experts and brands with whom we've collaborated.

There's more information on each of these brands in this guide.

Each of these brands excels in terms of delivering a great, high-quality product at a realistic price.

7. How do I know a CBD brand is trustworthy?

On the face of it, you don't. After all, pretty much anyone can throw up a website and start selling products.

OK, that's not 100% true, particularly if they are selling CBD oils, edibles or consumables, in which case their products do need to be recognised by the FSA and appear on their Novel Foods list (Check out the Resources section for a link).

However just because they're on the FSA list, that is not an automatic seal of approval in terms of being a trusted brand, with product quality and delivering value for money. Additionally, if they are only selling CBD balms or topicals they are exempt from the Food Standards Authority.

With all that said, your best way of reassuring yourself of your chosen brand's product quality is by doing some rudimentary research.

From our perspective, one of the first things we look for is a company or brand with a clearly communicated story, usually found on the About Us section of their website.

What we're looking for is a clear understanding of their proposition and transparency of who is actually behind the brand. We want to know the people behind the business. We want to know how and why they started the business and understand their motivations.

After all, the CBD industry is still a small market, where many of the businesses and brands are founded and led by passionate people who are honest and open.

We've found that having this level of transparency is a good indicator of a brand standing firmly behind its products.

So, what next?

8. What are CBD Lab Reports?

What are CBD Lab Reports and why are they important?

CBD lab reports are documents that provide detailed information about the quality and composition of a CBD product. They are also referred to as a Certificate of Analysis (COA) and are generated by independent laboratories based on samples of CBD sent for testing.

CBD lab testing is crucial because it ensures that the products consumers receive are accurately labelled and do in fact contain what the label says. They also provide accurate information on the other cannabinoids and compounds present within the product.

Having Lab Reports directly available on a CBD brand's website is not only a good sign in terms of quality assurance, but they serve a very important role in giving you precise information about the specific contents of a batch of CBD.

The Lab Reports will be specific to a batch of CBD and have a unique number. This number should directly correlate with the batch number shown on your CBD oil packaging or labelling. This means you can be sure of the exact composition of the CBD oil you're buying and ingesting.

As mentioned numerous times previously, not all CBD is created equally. Everything from the hemp seeds to the soil they're grown in, to the fertilisers used, right through to oil extraction, each of these processes in the production cycle will impact the quality and contents of the finished product.

So, the Lab Reports provide a great source of information and should be used to help inform your decision on which brand to buy from. CBD lab test report typically includes information about the cannabinoid profile of the product, including the levels of CBD, THC, CBG, CBN, and other cannabinoids. It may also include information about the terpene profile

This Lab Report should also identify any contaminants such as heavy metals, pesticides, and residual solvents. By comparing Lab Reports from a couple of different companies you'll be able to identify how different batches of CBD can vary - and more importantly, you can avoid anywhere there are higher levels of heavy metals or pesticides.

Some brands are much better than others in terms of transparency and visibility of their Lab Reports on their websites.

If their Reports are either hidden or non-existent, I would question the quality of the brand.

9. Which brands can I trust?

Hopefully you're now starting to get the picture about how to navigate your way through the complexities of the CBD market.

Unfortunately, it's not an easy or straightforward process and does mean you need to do your research.

This is a point that's reiterated by all our CBD Experts and is understandable given that you not only want to take something that's of good quality but also not excessively expensive and that will deliver the benefits you're looking for.

So, it's worthwhile doing your research and finding a brand you can really trust and stick with.

One of the quicker ways to do this research is through Reviews, although you should not rely exclusively on this approach.

With that said, given enough reviews, you can start to really get a feel for a company, not only in terms of the reviews they receive but also how the company responds to those reviews and feedback, both positively and negatively.

After all, it's often more about how a company responds to negative reviews that is more revealing in terms of their approach to quality assurance and customer service.

The easiest place to find and compare reviews across a range of CBD brands is to visit the Trust Pilot website and search for them there.

10. Am I getting value For money?

At the end of the day, if you've decided you're ready to try CBD for yourself and you've done some research and found some trusted brands, the only question that might still be a nagging doubt is the question of value for money.

And without actually trying a product and evaluating if you're getting the benefits you're seeking it's difficult to fully assess value for money. Because if you get the results, the chances are you'll think it's great value for money.

However, there is one metric you can use to help assess a number of different brands.

Firstly, you'll need to identify a range of brands that you believe are trusted and produce and market high-quality products.

Then if all those things are equal, the next thing you could look at is the cost per mg of CBD, as this can vary considerably from brand to brand.

With so many different strengths of CBD, packaged in different quantities (say gummies) or volumes (oils) it's often not instantly visible in terms of what you're paying per mg. And given all other things being equal, the price per mg of CBD is a significant factor in the value for money equation.

About six months ago we reviewed a range of 8 well-known brands of CBD gummies to see how they compared. The results were surprising. We found one brand in particular that was charging three times the price per mg of CBD.

So, once you're narrowed down your choice in terms of CBD brand, it's worth doing some quick calculations to see how they compare in terms of price per mg, to make sure you're getting the maximum value.

Three Things To Avoid:

Our final words of advice in terms of helping you navigate the CBD market in your search for the right CBD for you, we want to close with three things you should definitely avoid.

Buying from Garages or Petrol Stations

On one hand, it's great that CBD is becoming more widely understood and available not only online, but in specialist retailers and now even on the shelves of major supermarkets.

However, the appearance of CBD in some Garages and Petrol Stations is possibly cause for concern. Particularly when it's on sale for an almost unbelievable price.

As hopefully you've seen from everything we've written, the undeniable truth is that to a large extent you get what you pay for.

And if you're looking to consume CBD you wouldn't want to put anything in your body that was of poor quality, because the chances are you don't know what it contains and it's also unlikely to deliver the results you expect.

So when you see bottles of CBD oil at a fraction of the price you'd expect... avoid them.

CBD Oil In Clear Bottles

Another immediate concern would be to see CBD oil on sale in a clear bottle. The simple reason being that CBD degrades in sunlight, which dramatically impacts its potency and subsequent effectiveness. If you see CBD in a clear glass bottle, avoid it.

Medical Claims

As you probably already know, no brand or supplier of CBD products can make any medical claims around the use or consumption of CBD.

According to the MHRA, any CBD-containing products which are taken for medicinal purposes cannot make any medicinal claims which include the use of terms such as 'cure', 'restore', 'prevent', 'avoid', 'fight' or 'heal'. Also, it should go without saying, but claiming that a CBD product can treat cancer is prohibited by law.

So, if you come across a CBD brand or website that makes any sort of medical claim, avoid it.

With all that said, if you're still unsure what CBD to buy, we have a recommendation for you...

If you're new to CBD, or you've tried it before but not achieve the results or outcomes you were looking for, then this might be a good starting point for you.

We've teamed up with a small select number of CBD brands to bring you the best quality CBD products at the lowest price.

You can find out more on our website: **cbdgenie.uk/cbd-extra**

CBD eXtra

Visit our special website page:
www.cbdgenie.uk/cbd-extra
for details on a special offer we have for you

Or simply scan the QR code

SCAN ME

SECTION SIX:

CBD Stories

In this section we want to share a few personal experience stories of people using CBD. But, this is just the start, as we want to hear and share many more stories.

Why not join our CBD user community on Facebook?

Join the Facebook Group

Join our Facebook community and share your stories and experiences, as well as getting advice, tips and support: **cbdgenie.uk/facebook-group**

Or scan the QR code.

SCAN ME

Jonathan's 20-Year Sleep Struggle.

"Since starting our CBD journey, Matt and I have been looking at CBD products from different angles. I have suffered from poor sleep for 20 to 30 years, whether struggling to get to sleep or constantly waking up through the night".

Anybody who has suffered similar problems with their sleep will know that this can impact energy levels and productivity through the next day. It is debilitating!

So when we were sent some sample CBD from Kiara there was one which immediately caught my eye. It was their high-strength, 3000mg CBD oil, specifically formulated to help with sleep issues.

But can CBD oil help with sleep problems?

I'd previously tried one or two CBD products in the past without much success, so I was still looking for a real solution to my sleep problems.

However, when I'd taken CBD before I wasn't really aware of the different strengths and I'd been taking it in a rather haphazard way. So, this time I decided I needed a more structured and disciplined approach.

I started by taking 10 drops of the 3000mg oil each evening for about 30 minutes before going to bed. This works out to be around 50mg per dose, and bearing in mind the maximum recommended dose is 70mg per day, this is a high dose.

The way I calculated my initial dose level is by knowing that a 30ml bottle of CBD contains approximately 600 drops.

And given I was taking a 3000mg strength CBD, this meant each drop would contain 5mg of CBD.

I realise this goes against the convention of starting low and slowly building up your dose, but I was impatient to see if it was going to work at all. So my logic was that I'd start high to try and get a result, then slowly reduce my dose and hopefully still see the benefits.

Having taken a 50mg dose of CBD oil for a week, I finally got the result I was looking for.

There were four days out of the seven where I probably had the best quality sleep I'd had in years.

Waking, refreshed and ready to go.

It is difficult to explain the transformational impact of a good night's sleep. I suppose it is similar to somebody who suffers from arthritis; at some point, you begin to learn how to live with the condition.

For the last 20 to 30 years, due to my chronic sleep issues, I've learned to live with it, believing this to be the norm. As the working week progresses, I become increasingly tired.

By the end of the week, I am literally done!

Since we began the CBD Genie, we have tried several CBD products for different reasons. And whilst it's probably unfair to name other products, for me, Kiara is the only one which has made a noticeable difference.

However, this may be more to do with both the strength of dosage and me being more persistent in taking it, rather than something uniquely exceptional about their CBD.

Regardless, the change in my sleeping patterns, even at this early stage, has been remarkable.

What's the right dosage?

Having looked at many different CBD oils for sleep and spoken to people who have used them, one thing stands out, strength.

Initially, I tried 10mg and 20mg doses to help with my sleep, but this had no impact. This was disappointing, and I began to think that CBD wouldn't work for me.

Even though the 3000mg strength Kiara has worked for me, it didn't happen overnight, no pun intended!

It's only after having taken a constant dosage every day did I feel the benefit of cumulative doses. To put this into perspective, it wasn't until the third night that I felt the full benefits of an undisturbed night's sleep.

So, whether you are taking CBD oil for chronic sleeping issues, anxiety or pain relief, it is essential to appreciate that you might not feel the benefits immediately.

How and why does it work?

Now that I know the Kiara 3000mg strength CBD oil works for me, I need to look at tweaking the strength and dosage to find the optimum level.

After all, I may not need that high a dose, in which case I can definitely save money as the high-strength CBD oils aren't cheap.

While this might take some time and need adjusting along the way, the beauty is that I know which level definitely works for me.

However, I know that research has shown that the same levels of CBD will impact people differently.

Therefore, strength or dosage which works for a friend or partner may not have the same effect on you.

However, using trial and error, it is relatively easy to find the optimum level of CBD that works for you.

In summary:

Two main issues emerged for me during this test, which has been transformational for my sleeping pattern.

Firstly, it is essential that you find the right strength for yourself and don't dismiss CBD oil if it is not working straight away.

Secondly, you need to take a structured approach to CBD dosage so your body can build up the required levels.

I am pleased that I persevered even though I felt little impact for the first few days.

That feeling of relief, finally enjoying an undisturbed night's sleep, has been alien to me for 20 to 30 years.

What a difference CBD oil has made to my life!

Watch The Video

You can watch the interview on our YouTube channel **@cbdgenie**

or scan the QR code

SCAN ME

Jen's Journey To Pain-Free Living.

"I've been suffering from a range of aches and pains for a number of years, but recently they had become more noticeable, particularly when doing more physical work and DIY, which I love".

I started by occasionally taking a few CBD Gummies from Canax (their Sour Apple flavour).

Their gummies are quite large and each gummy has 25mg of CBD, so I felt I was getting a reasonable dose.

My initial reaction to these was very encouraging, with a noticeable reduction in pain and also greater flexibility of movement, so I decided I wanted to give them a proper try.

I then tried the strawberry flavour Gummies and while they were nice, I prefer the sour apple Gummies from a taste perspective.

However, when they ran out, I stopped taking any CBD for at least a month.

Was the CBD really making a difference?

I do a lot of DIY work and practical stuff which can involve heavy lifting. I'm a very physical person and injured my arm last year which was really beginning to have an affect on me.

Also, I exercise regularly, and my daughter had recently noticed a clicking and crunching sound in my knee joints, all sort of age-related and obvious wear and tear.

Anyway, the pain had become almost constant, until I started taking the Gummies. Then it really just stopped hurting, which was sort of a bit unbelievable.

How quickly did it take effect?

I would say the CBD started taking effect after about a week and I noticed that my body was making fewer noises. There was less clicking and crunching during and after exercising.

I know that some people are taking CBD for anxiety. While I don't find myself to be a particularly anxious person, I can occasionally get stressed about things.

Since starting with the Gummies, if I need to chill a bit, I will have one and it does that. It chills me down.

What happened when I stopped taking them?

I stopped taking them for a while so that I could be sure that it was actually the Gummies which were helping with my aches and pains.

But within a week of me stopping taking them, my aches and pains started to come back.

My initial thought was that it may be a coincidence, and perhaps I was just getting better anyway. But now I know it's down to the Gummies, and I always make sure I have some in the house.

How many CBD Gummies did it take?

I tend to just take one a day but sometimes I might skip a day if I'm feeling quite good.

I have never had anything with CBD in it before, so this was my first time. And I am not taking anything else in terms of medication or supplements, so I can say hand on heart that the way I feel is because they're working.

I also like the fact that Canax does sugar-free Gummies which are great if you don't want any sugar.

These are just like little bears, they are perfect if you are going out and you can just stick a few in a little pot.

I have to say that I'm now a CBD convert!

Watch The Video

You can watch the interview on our YouTube channel **@cbdgenie**

or scan the QR code

SCAN ME

Guitarist Andy's Arthritic Fingers.

I've always been active, playing sports, particularly tennis and cricket to a relatively high standard in my youth. As I've grown older, my joints have begun to ache, and I've developed arthritis in both my knees and my hands.

It's not debilitating (yet!), but flare-ups can be agonising and last anything from a couple of weeks, up to three months. It's particularly bad when my knees flare up as walking becomes difficult and very painful.

And the arthritis in my fingers has meant I've had to almost re-learn how to play guitar, finding work-arounds as I've lost much of my dexterity in my fingers.

Being someone who's played the guitar since I was 15 and currently still regularly playing in pub bands, this has been particularly hard and frustrating.

Over the last six months or so I've tried a number of things to reduce or alleviate the pain, including significant changes to my diet and lifestyle – basically cutting out all the unhealthy stuff and getting regular exercise.

But despite this, I still experience these flare-ups in my knees, and arthritis in my fingers has got progressively worse so it's hard to grip things and clenching my fist is impossible.

So when I approached Matt and Jonathan I was open to trying anything.

I had already read quite a bit about CBD and its potential to help with arthritis, so I was curious and eager to try it.

Starting slow and steady

To kick things off we agreed to take a structured approach so we could try and identify if the CBD specifically was helping, or possibly other factors.

It wasn't exactly a scientific approach, but we did have a clear plan.

I started with CBD gummies, taking just one 12mg gummy a day for about 5 days. Then I increased the dose to one 25mg gummy a day for the next 5 days.

However I didn't see much of a difference in my pain levels during that time.

At this point I was starting to feel a little sceptical and wondered if CBD was more hype than reality in terms of actually making a difference.

Time to go large

Given I'd had no response to the lower doses, we then decided I should now try the high strength gummies, at 69mg per gummy – again taking just one a day.

This is when things started to change.

I noticed I could get out of bed more easily and my joints didn't ache as much.

And during the two or three weeks I took the gummies, I only experienced two flare-ups, both of which were significantly shorter than usual, lasting only a couple of days – and were less painful.

Was it really the CBD?

I couldn't say for 100% certainty the CBD was responsible for these improvements, but I couldn't deny that the overall achiness seemed to be significantly reduced. The pain from flare-ups was still there, but it seemed to go away more quickly than it had in the past.

However, what happened next did convince me more.

I went on a five day trip to Spain with friends, but I didn't take the gummies with me. After just a few days I noticed that my joints started to ache more and getting out of bed was more painful.

When I got back home I immediately started back on the gummies and once again the pain subsided even when I started increasing my physical activity.

Before trying the CBD gummies, I had never used CBD before. As someone who has an ailment, I felt partly converted to the idea of using CBD to manage my pain.

From cynic to convert

I've always had a positive mindset about the potential benefits of CBD, and my experience with the gummies has further solidified that belief.

I'm now looking to try other forms of CBD and in particular the CBD oils, to see if they might offer even more relief for my arthritis pain, particularly for my hands.

I know I still have good days and bad days, but if I continue to see improvements in my pain levels and flare-up frequency, I'll be more convinced that CBD is the way to go.

As a cynic, I'll always be honest about my experiences. So far, I can tentatively say that CBD seems to be working for me. I'll need more time to be 100% sure, but I'm excited to continue exploring the potential benefits of CBD for my arthritis.

Watch The Video

You can watch the interview on our You Tube channel **@cbdgenie**

or scan the QR code

SCAN ME

In Summary...

Writing and collating this book has been a journey where we have learnt so much, and realised just how much there is still to learn.

We've drafted and re-drafted each section to avoid, we hope, making things too complicated or chewy.

At the beginning we set out to share our journey and attempt to open up the world of CBD to those who largely know little about it and help navigate their choices towards the products which will suit them.

The route to finding an effective solution to your healthcare needs with CBD is definitely not a one size fits all. It's about tailoring it to your own personal circumstances and biology.

We really hope that this book has proved a useful guide and even if it hasn't definitively answered the question 'Will it work for me?' we hope that it has given some clarity on exactly how you can find out!

We look forward to hearing how your journey goes!

Matthew Burch and Jonathan Howkins, CBD Genie.

Write a Review

You can leave your review by visiting:
cbdgenie.uk/book-review
or simply scan the QR code to visit our website where you'll find full details.

Thank you - we really do appreciate you taking the time to do this.

SCAN ME

SECTION SEVEN

References & Resources

Listed below are a number of additional resources you can use to learn more about CBD and the industry and regulation that surrounds it.

FSA (Food Standards Agency)
https://www.food.gov.uk

MHRA (Medicines and Healthcare products Regulatory Agency)
https://www.gov.uk/government/organisations/
medicines-and-healthcare-products-regulatory-agency

Association for the Cannabinoid Industry
https://theaci.co.uk

The UK Cannabis Trades Association
https://cannabistrades.uk

CMC (Centre for Medicinal Cannabis)
https://thecmcuk.org

British Hemp Alliance
https://britishhempalliance.co.uk

The Cannabis Industry Council
https://cannabisindustrycouncil.co.uk

The CBD and Cannabis Professional Network
https://www.cannapro-uk.org

CLEAR. Cannabis Law Reform
https://clearmembers-uk.org

European Industrial Hemp Association (EIHA)
https://eiha.org

NICE (National Institute for Health and Care Excellence)
https://www.nice.org.uk

NHS (National Health Service)
https://www.nhs.uk

BMA (British Medical Association)
https://www.bma.org.uk

Drug Science
https://drugscience.org.uk

The British Pain Society
https://www.britishpainsociety.org

Arthritis Research UK
https://www.versusarthritis.org

MS Society
https://www.mssociety.org.uk

British Epilepsy Association
https://www.epilepsy.org.uk

CBD Intel
https://www.cbd-intel.com

The Cannavist Magazine
https://www.thecannavistmag.com

Hemp & CBD Media
https://www.hempandcbdmedia.com

Leafie
https://www.leafie.co.uk

More Resources

We'll continue to update our list of useful resources here:
www.cbdgenie.uk/resources

or scan the QR code.

Let's Keep In Touch

Throughout this guide we've added links and QR codes to additional content and resources which we hope you've found interesting and helpful.

But if you've any specific questions you'd like to ask, then we'd love to hear from you. You can contact us via any of our social media channels or using the Contact Us page on our website.

Additionally we look forward to hearing from you in our **CBD Facebook Group** (cbdgenie.uk/facebook-group)

We hope this will be an active and dynamic community where everyone can help and support each other, as well as share their own experiences and CBD stories.

As we said at the start of this book, we too are on a CBD journey and look forward to being able to share more with you as our journey continues.

Join the Facebook Group

Join our Facebook community and share your stories and experiences, as well as getting advice, tips and support: **cbdgenie.uk/facebook-group**

Or scan the QR code.

SCAN ME

BVRSH - #0001 - 160523 - C2 - 229/152/10 - PB - 9781739387501 - None Lamination